The Art of Love
The Craft of Relationship

If love is the art, then relationship
is the craft of being in life together

The Art of Love
The Craft of Relationship

A Practical Guide for Creating the Loving Relationships We Want

Bud Harris, Ph.D.
&
Massimilla Harris, Ph.D.

Fisher King Press

www.fisherkingpress.com

info@fisherkingpress.com

+1-831-238-7799

Distributed by
Fisher King Books
PO Box 222321
Carmel, CA 93922
+1-831-238-7799
1-800-228-9316 Toll Free Canada & USA

CONTENTS

A FEW OPENING WORDS

For one human being to love another human being: that is perhaps the most difficult task that has been entrusted to us, the ultimate task, the final test and proof, the work for which all other work is merely preparatory.

—Rainer Maria Rilke

Falling in love is magical. We feel as if we know each other in ways that no one else has ever known us, and that we are cherished because (or in spite) of who we are. We believe that our love will last forever, that we will overcome the problems and pitfalls of tradition, chance, or circumstances to beat the odds and to live happily together.

But as daily life takes over, our frustration and disappointment often builds. We try hard to return to the magical way things once were; we all long for love and do not want to be alone. As our passion fades away under the weight of complicated lives, the air we once breathed from the high places where we imagine love comes from becomes stale and stagnant. Our love can become obscured by apathy or power struggles. If we are totally honest, thoughts of giving up, or ways of escaping our pain creep uneasily into our minds.

Our approach to better relationships is not to "work on" them but to acquire the skills that help us to develop them. This is more than a book. It is a guide to help us learn what real love feels like, what it is like to truly care and feel cared for, and what it is like to have a love you can trust. It feels great to know you have been there for a partner when they really needed you. So does knowing he or she will be there for you. In over six decades of combined practice, we have seen repeatedly that most people have not reached this level in their relationships, not because they did not want to, but because they simply did not know how.

Through our own efforts at creating a fulfilling life together, we have learned that love can become the guiding principle of our lives and that even through struggles, tears, illness, crisis, and loss, we can count on a firm foundation of peace to support us. As Massimilla and I continue on our journey, we have made a commitment to share what we have learned with the people we counsel so that they, too, can discover that the tools we teach restore us personally as they restore our relationships. With the right map and equipment, new growth and deeper love can be generated through—especially through—obstacles and crises.

We may know what we want, but we have had no new designs and few guidelines to help us create the kind of relationships we seek. With this book, we hope to change that. In our work with couples, in crisis or transition, we are struck by the relief many feel once they realize that being stuck or struggling does not mean that they are failing.

Common wisdom tells us that the only thing constant in our life is change. It is as natural and necessary for us to grow and change as it is for a butterfly to emerge from a cocoon. And so as analysts, we find it helpful to use the metaphor of a journey to show how a relationship must evolve if it is going to fulfill our hopes and needs as we progress through our lives.

For decades we have used the journey image to help couples transform their relationship in ways that nurture the growth of love and intimacy. We have designed our seminars to help people map out the journey of creating and re-creating a loving relationship. We all have the journey in common. But every journey is as separate, singular, and unique as the people making it. We have a lot to teach and a lot to learn from each other. That's why we are inviting you, in this book, to join one of our seminars as both an observer and a participant.

First, we will explain the format of our seminars and introduce you to the five couples who are participating in this particular one. Then we will listen to a story about love's journey that will serve as one type of roadmap for how we can grow together. We know that love always takes us somewhere. It can send us into the rapture of heaven or into the hell of despair. While we may not have control over the direction our journey takes at times, we do have control over what we learn. Even journeys to hell have meaning if we seek to understand what they are trying to teach us.

Insights and know-how for undertaking and understanding our own journey will emerge as we move between the myth, personal stories, an illustrative story, and our perspective as analysts. We will explore intimacy skills, what it means that opposites attract, how to face our fears, and how to decide what changes we can ask of our partners. (Yes, we can ask our partners to change and even insist on it at times.) These skills provide us with valuable relationship tools we can use to effectively handle more difficult or threatening problems.

It is important to remember that if a relationship is a journey, as life is, then problems and their solutions are only bumps, or temporary detours, along the way. How we handle those problems—from sex to stepchildren—and what we learn from the process are often more important to our relationships than the actual solution to the problems. If we feel that we have been listened to, understood, and respected, we feel valued and loved. If we feel bullied, hurt, or coerced, then the relationship has been wounded, *even if a particular problem has been solved*. That's why we need to learn the craft of relationship. The skills to understand and handle problems help us build our relationships, while "expert" answers may contribute little to the growth of our lives together.

When Massimilla and I begin a seminar by explaining that we no longer have a model for relationships, we always feel a collective release of tension in the room. As we share the story of love's journey, using the classic myth of Eros and Psyche as our example, interest and enthusiasm builds. Once we have heard the story, we discuss it and see what the events in it mean to us, and how we can apply them in our lives. When we move into our exploration of the craft of relationships, the energy in the room intensifies. Participants become engaged in a way that brings a spirit of hope and buoyancy to the process.

To be secure with someone you trust, to feel loved, respected, and to be able to talk openly, sharing troubles and joys, is a mark of true intimacy. To be in life together this way, we must learn the craft of intimate communication. Each lesson we learn, or skill we master, is a step in this direction. And, when we discover how to face our fears, it frees our ability to live with love, and to learn how to see and deal with our stumbling blocks, limited perspectives, and needs in a new way. It is rejuvenating to learn that relationships call us to grow into our best potentials, to learn to trust, to be intimate, and to cherish how other people are different from us.

Recognizing our uniqueness fuels the development of our best relationships. Learning how to bridge our differences and appreciate each other's uniqueness brings trust and excitement to our lives. Plus, it puts us on the path of learning the craft of relationship—a path that will help life flow, even through difficult times, and will help us fall in love again and again as our shared lives unfold.

Our goal for ourselves, for those who seek our help, and for you is to experience relationships as a structure where love flourishes, suffering and resentment releases its grip, and life becomes a lot more enjoyable.

We hope that you enjoy what you discover, or are reminded of, in these pages. And, that your discovery brings a new spirit to your willingness to participate in one of life's most important commitments: the craft of being in life together, in love.

PART ONE

THE ART OF LOVE

Lovers begin by frolicking near the shore in the shallow waters of desire, but the currents of time sweep them toward the oceanic depths, where the mystery of being, freedom and creation is 10,000 fathoms deep.

—Sandor McNab

1

THE SEMINAR

*Love doesn't just sit there, like a stone, it has to be made like bread;
remade all of the time, made new.*

—Ursula LeGuinn

On a Saturday morning in late spring my wife, Massimilla, and I are joined by five couples attending our four-Saturday relationship seminar. This number of people is small enough for us to get to know one another, yet large enough to include a variety of different situations, perspectives, and life experiences from which to learn. While each couple brings their own unique struggle to the seminar, we have found that most couples have a few fears in common: fear of being overwhelmed; fear of being rejected and abandoned; fear of not being appreciated and loved; fear of having to sacrifice their uniqueness to keep the waters of the relationship calm, and; fear of losing their fantasy image or the ideal of the relationship. We always keep these kinds of fears in mind. But we have discovered that by the end of the learning process in the seminar, the participants usually have grown far beyond their initial fears and challenges.

We will now introduce the couples, explain why they are here, and what they hope to gain from the seminar.

Bob and Trish, a couple in their mid-forties, are both married for the second time, and both have children from their former marriages. Their specific challenge is that they fear being overwhelmed by the busyness of a blended family, of being abandoned by the other because the new family is too much work, and a deep, lurking fear of the shame of failing again. They want more trust, ease, and fulfilling intimacy in their relationship.

Our next couple, Tom and Cindy, might be thought of as more traditional. They have been married for eighteen years and have two children in high school. They share a fear that their marriage won't last for the long term, and they also fear failure and being alone. Tom is afraid because of his father's failed marriages and Cindy is afraid because she was unrecognized and loved for who she was in her family of origin. They hope to gain a sense of security and confidence in their ability to stay committed and satisfied long-term.

Our third couple is Barry and Cory. They are in their mid-thirties, and have two small children. They both realize their lives have become busy and complicated and their relationship is becoming stale. Plus, they have lost the deep feeling of understanding each other that they once shared. They would like to rekindle their deep connection, and learn how to prioritize their relationship so it doesn't get lost in the daily chaos.

Karen and Leah are a gay couple in their mid-thirties who have been together about a year. They are afraid bad moods and the ups and downs of life will threaten the ideal fantasy of the relationship they long for, and for which they have never seen a model. They hope to better understand the healthy cycles in a relationship, and to more deeply trust each other.

Our youngest couple is Michael and Vanessa. They are in their early thirties and have been living together for four years. Both come from families in which the parents solidified into roles while building up anger and resentment under the thin veneer of happy appearances. They are afraid marriage could be the beginning of the end of their relationship. They most want to learn to be true to themselves while learning to honor and accept each other's differences.

Once everyone is seated, Massimilla and I begin by taking a few minutes to explain how modern life has eroded and confused our expectations of how we should live together. As our social and cultural institutions have changed, our relationships to work, religion, community, and to our own families have also shifted. The advent of birth control, women's rights, a high divorce rate, and living in a fearful, fast-moving, bottom-line-oriented culture have robbed us of the traditions and communities that either gave us, or enforced, stability in our lives. Jobs, families, sex, security, and the future have become more uncertain than they were even a generation ago. We face multiple careers, blended marriages, and new styles of relationships while often having grown up in broken or dysfunctional homes. Each one of our couples faces difficult challenges, and is looking for a kind of fulfillment their grandparents would not have been able to articulate.

We have become pioneers once again, mapping out new territory for the relationships we now live. However, we point out that blazing new trails does not mean one has to throw out important personal values that have been developed. In fact, the journey of growing together often renews our sensitivity to, and respect for, our deeper values, and the more we learn to love, the more we appreciate all of the wonder life offers.

As the seminar proceeds, I˙ share some of my own story. My generation grew into adulthood in the 1950s and saw marriage as a signpost pointing toward maturity. I got married in order to seal my passage into adult life. It was a respectable way to define myself and begin a life I thought would be rewarding. I believed love and marriage automatically went together and if I lived responsibly, love would expand and endure. As it endured, I thought love would make my life easier, more stable, and more complete. Instead, day-to-day married life proved to make my life more complicated, troubling, and, challenging. Yet in spite of this rocky start, I was to learn, in ways that I could not have imagined when I was young, how the art of love and the craft of relationship would make my life more mature, whole, and fulfilling.

I eventually discovered that my desire to get married, and the manner in which I was trying to love, had more to do with fulfilling what I thought my role was in a way that appeared successful than it had to do with how I truly felt. This inconsistency compelled me to begin to look at love and relationships, in my personal *and* professional lives, as forces that either allow us to face our deeper needs and desires, and move more confidently into the deeper waters of true intimacy in relationship. Or as forces that can strip us of joy and vitality, which often happens, when we are struggling to grow and mature.

Massimilla, through a very different journey, came to a similar conclusion. She was raised a family where a woman was expected to marry and emotionally support her husband and children. Her family and community regarded a woman's education and personal ambitions as secondary. If she worked at all, it was only to contribute to the family's support. She found these models of adulthood and relationships in her early life inadequate. As a result, she spent many years struggling to define the values and ideals that would support her efforts to have an authentic life she could claim as her own.

˙ To avoid redundant author identification, the "I" will refer to Bud unless otherwise noted.

Massimilla and I met and married in mid-life after our previous relationships failed. Yet even though they failed, they became vital catalysts for our personal and professional growth. Our stories reflect challenges and triumphs that are deeply personal and intensely experienced. However, considered from a wider perspective, our experiences may be seen as two waves in a greater sea that compels the kind of personal growth that ultimately allows relationships to flourish. This sea holds not only cultural dissatisfaction and change, conflict and facing new dilemmas, but also growth, maturity, wisdom, and true intimacy. We all are witnesses and participants in this sea of fluctuating values, expectations, and experience. Massimilla and I are committed to sharing the hard-won lessons we both have learned in our lives and work with people in this seminar, in our practice, and with our readers.

In Their Own Words

We now ask everyone to introduce himself or herself and share briefly why they are here. We have found this to be a good way to begin to get to know each other.

Bob and Trish, the couple with the blended family, are the first to talk. Looking a bit imposing because of his size, Bob stands large and tells us in a gruff voice, even as he looks at the floor, that he is there because some of their friends told them that this seminar helped them better understand their relationship. He admits that he doesn't understand his relationship with Trish. "Trish is mad all of the time. So I guess this is worth a try." In the beginning, his skeptical attitude rarely leaves him.

Trish, a blonde, petite woman of about the same age with lively eyes and a quick smile, seems the opposite of her husband. She counters Bob's assessment by telling us that she is not mad all of the time. Her smile fades as she adds, "But I am often frustrated. Bob has two teenagers that spend every other weekend with us. I have a son and a daughter in middle school who visit their Dad occasionally, but live with us. All of the coming and going, school events, and ball games make me feel like I'm living in a circus. Bob just ignores it, so I'm left being the ring master, managing everybody's schedule, and wondering when we're going to have some time together to just sit and talk." She pauses and then admits, "I am mad. We have got to learn how to run our lives instead of being run by our children's schedules." She ends with an important request: she wants some support in feeling like their relationship is important to Bob.

They are followed by Tom and Cindy, who have been married since college. Tom has the look of an athlete and speaks with confidence. "Our daughters are in high school and we are facing being alone together in a few years. I think it will be a chance for us to get to know each other again, or actually even better." The confidence in his voice seems to falter.

Cindy, who appears more reserved and thoughtful, responds that she agrees with Tom. She, too, would like for them to get to know each other again. She hesitates, and then adds, "But we're really different. Tom likes the outdoors—jogging, hiking and mountain biking—and I don't. He's outgoing and I like being at home. For years I admired his energy, but secretly felt that because I couldn't match it, I had less to offer our relationship." She explained that as she has grown to appreciate herself more, she is better able to see that they have been drifting apart slowly for a long time. "I'm worried about how we can bridge some of these differences and regain our closeness," she admits, glancing at Tom. "We've had so many friends separate or divorce lately, I am a little scared."

From the nods and murmurs of assent from others in the room, we recognize that she has touched on a common fear.

Barry and Cory go next. Their two small children are the main focus in their lives. "Before the boys came along, I was a banker and I like order," Cory begins. "As much as I love being at home with them, they are so demanding and tireless, I often feel overwhelmed."

"Two little guys definitely let you know the honeymoon is over," Barry adds, in support of Cory's assessment. He goes on to express that he thinks they need to regain some of the intimacy they felt at the beginning of their marriage, even if it is only for a few minutes here and there. He adds that it is too easy to get tired and frustrated and then take it out on each other. "Cory blew up at me when I bought new speakers for the stereo and I got so mad at her I realized we could use some help."

Massimilla and I are always struck by the candor and courage couples bring to our seminars. This group is no exception.

Karen and Leah introduce themselves next. They are struggling to work out a long-term committed relationship. Karen is a tall, imposing blonde woman; Leah is a smaller, trim, and intense woman. Karen begins by acknowledging that they want to learn how to keep intimacy alive in an unsupportive world. Leah adds, in a humorous voice, "We certainly don't have many successful models, so it's good to hear nobody else does either."

Good-natured laughter comes from several people around the room.

"We're worried for many of the same reasons as Barry and Cory. It's too easy to get angry and defensive when we're stressed," she concludes.

The final couple to speak are Michael and Vanessa. Our youngest couple, they are living together but afraid to get married. Vanessa has short black hair, a slightly round figure, and deep brown eyes. Michael is wiry, with clear blue eyes, and full of nervous energy.

"We need help," Vanessa articulates with an engaging smile. Then, more serious, she continues by explaining that her parents divorced when she was fourteen, and Michael's mother has been angry with his father for as long as Michael can remember. She speaks for them both when she says that they want to do better than their parents did, but they feel discouraged. "Most of our friends don't seem to know how to make a commitment work either," she finishes, with sadness in her voice.

"We love each other," Michael interjects, "but it looks like once you make the long-term commitment, things go downhill fast. People get tense and seem to forget about love. I guess it's safe to say we're scared, too."

Massimilla affirms their honest disclosures by acknowledging that being able to admit fears and ask for help is a good beginning.

We consistently find that the diversity of issues in our seminars, like the fresh struggles of Karen and Leah, and Michael and Vanessa, as well as the complications of young children, such as those being experienced by Barry and Cory, remind us of the difficulties relationships go through from the beginning. The problems of older children in a relationship, such as Bob's and Trish's, the experiences of failed relationships, and the need to find the courage to begin again underline how important it is to learn more about the craft of creating a loving, lasting relationship. Yet in spite of such seeming diversity, the similarities we share help us to more fully appreciate what we all have in common: our need and desire for sustainable love and intimacy.

The Importance of Story

After a small break, Massimilla introduces the story we are going to use, an adaptation of the ancient Greek myth of Eros and Psyche. We regard this myth as a turning point in the history of Western love. It is one of the earliest stories that illustrates love as a journey into growth and joy, rather than as a state of possession that grips our lives and then abandons us in the throes of our obligations, duties, and responsibilities.

Myths offer insights to better understand our lives because they reveal the larger patterns underlying them. These stories help us to view our personal problems through new eyes, and help us to remember that our issues and challenges are universal. Myths also shed light on some of the unconscious foundations of our feelings, and motivations for our actions. By paying attention to the story, we often are able to better orient ourselves. By seeing ourselves at some point in the story line, we may relate to, and better understand, the potential we are striving to live into.

The story of Eros and Psyche clarifies some of the ups and downs in this journey called love, while opening the door to an awareness that the love we share with another can expand our souls, and bring meaning and fulfillment into our lives. The myth of Eros and Psyche describes a pattern lived by two lovers. Yet there is a story within the story because Psyche is the Greek word for "soul," and Eros is the Greek word for "love." On a deeper level, the story reveals how the love that grows between two people is reflected in the trials and conflicts that we each must first face within ourselves. Equally important, it demonstrates how these trials can strengthen us, and increase our capacity to love.

A story-within-a-story can also be confusing. One minute we may find our experiences with our partner following the plot proper of the story, and the next minute the plot may turn inward and seem to be describing our efforts to find love within ourselves. It may be helpful to read the story several times in order to see which parts stand out in a new way each time, and to determine the ways in which it is personally relevant. Next, we will briefly introduce and describe the main characters, present the story, and then discuss some of our responses to the story.

Our Invisible Partners

The four major characters depicted in this story represent often-hidden parts that reside within us all. They may influence or take over our lives without our even recognizing them. For example, we may find ourselves like Eros, wanting love without risk, and without having to reveal ourselves. Or we may find ourselves seized by a mood that leaves us criticizing everything about our partner, which means we have been taken over by Psyche's sisters. All of the parts, visible and invisible, within each of us have an important role in the development of our relationships. Maturity asks us to cultivate enough self-awareness to recognize the patterns in our lives and relationships. Doing so makes us more confident, helps us to understand and accept gloomy times, and enhances our ability to make growthful choices for our relationships.

Regardless of where we find ourselves in the story, we must learn how to transform attraction into love, and love into growth and joy.

Eros and Psyche: The players

Aphrodite: The goddess of attraction and lust. She gets life moving, but then wants to keep us from growing beyond our passions and fantasies.

Eros: The son of Aphrodite who wants love without risk, without having to reveal himself, or having to see his lover in daylight.

Psyche: A beautiful princess who wants to be loved in reality, not as a fantasy.

Psyche's Sisters: Jealous, moody, and critical sisters who create restlessness and dissatisfaction, but who also, paradoxically, keep life moving.

2

THE STORY:
A MAP FOR THE JOURNEY

These are the stories that never die, that are carried like seed into a new country, are told to you and me and make in us new and lasting strengths.

—Meridel LeSueur

This is the story* from long ago that begins while the beautiful princess Psyche is having trouble finding a partner. Because Psyche had become so famous for her beauty, she intimidated many of her suitors. In the meantime, her less attractive sisters have found husbands, and Psyche's parents are wringing their hands out of concern for her future. They cannot understand why Psyche has received no offers for marriage.

In the same way Psyche's suitors felt, the opportunity for an exceptional, surprising relationship may actually frighten us. Deep inside we may doubt whether we are truly lovable, deserving, or can live up to such beauty.

But this is not Psyche's only problem. She does not trust her own attractiveness and this makes her suspicious of her suitors, wondering if they are interested to know who she really is. Yet beneath the attractive surface of her life, Psyche feels lonely, even though she does not quite know what she herself wants from a relationship. She does know that she does not want to settle for the shallow kind of marriages that her sisters have. She wants to be loved for who she is, and is tired of being praised and admired by people who are so awed by her appearance that they cannot feel comfortable with, or truly know, her.

---

* This chapter contains my abbreviated narration of the myth for our study and discussion. See Appendix A for an additional narrative.

Both Psyche's beauty and her unwillingness to settle for an ordinary relationship anger the goddess of attraction, Aphrodite. In a rage, Aphrodite sends her son Eros, the god of love, to dispose of Psyche by making her fall in love with a monster. However, as soon as Eros sees Psyche, he falls in love with her. While she sleeps, he gently carries her to his home.

Psyche awakens to find herself in a beautiful home with rich surroundings. She is filled with wonder and fear at the same time. But life proceeds well. Eros comes to her every night and, in the dark, hidden from sight, they enjoy their love. Life seems like paradise. However, when Psyche seeks to know him better, and wants to share his company in the light of day, he refuses. He tells her it will destroy their happy life together. Before long, Psyche becomes lonely and invites her sisters to visit. They are jealous of Psyche's happiness and begin to ask her questions about what kind of person her partner is. "Isn't this all too good to be true?" "How do you know he's not really a monster?" "How can you trust his love if you don't really know him?" "What will happen if times get tough; will he leave you for good?"

Eventually these questions, fear, and her own curiosity convince Psyche she should try to see Eros. One night she waits until Eros was asleep. Then carrying a lamp and a knife in case he really was a monster, she sheds the lamplight on his sleeping body and looks at him. While she is standing there, transfixed by his beauty, oil from her lamp spills on Eros, burning and awakening him. With a cry of despair he leaves Psyche, saying he can never return.

Our story has now revealed a common theme in relationships: no matter how initially strong or how pleasing, we *will* experience a crisis in love. Whether we are first drawn to our partner by a strong attraction, mutual need, or deep friendship, we approach new relationships full of hope, anticipating happiness and security. Then when love is eclipsed by the pain of conflict and unmet needs, it may seem as if our hopes are dashed against the earth as soon as we encounter this pain and difficulty. When our relationships do not seem to work or meet our expectations, we become angry with ourselves, and with our partners. We blame and berate ourselves for being so stupid to have become so vulnerable, admonish ourselves for failing, or we withdraw after convincing ourselves that love is just an illusion anyway.

The truth is Psyche had not made a mistake. A crisis or conflict is both a time of danger *and* of opportunity. If we brave the danger and choose the path of opportunity, conflict—rather than signaling the end—can become a turning point.

I pause to emphasize this first essential lesson:

Crisis = Turning Point

Psyche's restless questions and her need to know Eros better was actually her need to grow and this is a natural and healthy stage in relationships. We first need to feel bonded as lovers, almost part of each other. Then we have to separate in order to see our partner "in the daylight," as he or she really is, beneath the way we have idealized him or her. And, by returning to ourselves, we can see ourselves clearly, reclaiming our personal sense of values and strengths, weaknesses, hopes, and desires. Then we can build a new foundation that gives love a chance to grow to a new level. A place where we can seek to know and love our partners more completely as they truly are, rather than simply wanting to be happy with them. We can grow together as a couple without selling ourselves out in an effort to avoid change. In other words, we have just learned that it takes two whole people to be in life together.

Such a crisis may leave us feeling sad, scared, and abandoned. It also confronts us with the choice of whether or not to withdraw from the relationship, literally or figuratively, or to begin the process of trying to repair and renew it. Eros withdrew from the relationship, burned and suffering, and Psyche was left in such despair that she wondered whether or not life was worth living. None of the other gods or goddesses would help them at first because they were afraid of offending Aphrodite, who was jealous of Psyche. When we are devastated by love, we, too, may feel there is little help available. Rationality, power, money, talent, potential, and even anger often seem useless, only adding to our feelings of emptiness. But in the myth, there was one exception. The nature god, Pan, comforted Psyche and urged her to search for Eros. In other words, it is part of our nature to search for love and growth no matter how bad we feel—and eventually we can find help within ourselves.

The process of upsetting our relationship in order to know our partner better, and to reclaim our own standpoint can be discouraging because we have been taught that a crisis conflicts with the ideals we hold about living happily together. But if our relationship and love is to be continually re-created, it is helpful to understand the process the story is unfolding. Their experiences of coming apart and then seeking and returning to each other are natural and happen in ways, large and small, as they pass through the different stages of life. Their story can help us locate similar patterns in our own lives; and while they may be painful, if we recognize them for what they are, they are less likely to destroy our love.

We learn that living happily ever after is not the same as living happily together. In the naive storybook scenario of living happily ever after, this phrase ends the story: it is over. In the second situation, living happily together, the story continues chapter after chapter, just like life.

Let us note the second essential lesson from the story:

Love = Growth

When Eros said he would never return, this illustrates the reality that our relationship can never return to its original state of bliss. But this does not mean it should be abandoned.

> *Finally, another goddess tells Psyche, who has now discovered she is pregnant, that in order to find Eros, she must first confront Aphrodite and reconcile with her. And though Psyche thought she wanted to see Eros in the daylight, she did not realize how drastically this would affect their relationship, and how much she would have to grow in order for their love to live into its next chapter.*

Facing Aphrodite and coming to terms with her means that Psyche must accept the difficult job of understanding that the fantasies and expectations our attractions generate are not going to match the upcoming reality of a real relationship. Yet, as the end of the story illustrates, if we accept this fact, continue to value love and attraction, and persevere in our efforts to grow, our outcomes can be far better than our fantasies. Learning to enjoy attraction without imprisoning it with our expectations is an important part of the craft of relationship. This awareness can often help us resist the impulse to close down in order to protect ourselves emotionally.

Psyche bravely undertakes the tasks of reconciliation assigned by Aphrodite. In the first task, she must sort out a huge pile of mixed seeds before sunset.

This task reminds us of how carefully we have to sort through our confused thoughts and feelings, no matter how overwhelming or impossible it may seem.

Her second task is to collect a sample of golden fleece from one of the sun god's rams, which goes dangerously mad at the sight of a person.

Here Psyche learns to act creatively with courage in the service of love.

Her third task is to collect a small urn of water from the river Styx, which separates the realm of the living from that of the dead. To touch this water is fatal.

Yet the Styx is the river of life and Psyche is learning that she must meet life patiently and carefully without grasping for too much too quickly.

Her final task is to get a box of beauty cream from Persephone, the queen of the underworld. Persephone's realm lies beyond the river Styx and its entrance is guarded by the three-headed dog, Cerberus.

Beauty sought from the queen of darkness helps us understand how wrong our culture is to teach us that the pursuit of beauty will bring happiness and the absence of conflict; that beauty holds a danger that only can be conquered with the power of love. Many of our dark moments, those in which we feel pain, despair, loneliness, and failure, are the ones that teach us the most about the true nature of love and highlight true turning points in our growth.

Yet Psyche does not labor alone. She is assisted at these tasks by nature, fate, and the gods. Ants come to her and help to sort the seeds. Reeds by the river whisper to her to wait for the rams to pass and pick some of the fleece left on the brambles. The eagle of Zeus fills her urn from the river Styx. And finally, when she is almost overcome by despair and is about to throw herself off a tower, the tower speaks to her. It explains how she can prepare three cakes to placate Cerberus, find Persephone, and safely return.

We, too, can find help when we work at the tasks required for our growth. Our friends and relatives, books and counselors, among other resources, become available as a result of our efforts and our sincere desire to grow and change.

It is important to realize that Psyche's tasks were not punishments. In order to set her journey in motion, she, like the rest of us, first must fall in love before she can learn how to enjoy love without losing herself in it. The tasks are necessary for her growth into maturity, for the ability to discern her feelings and potentials, to find support and strength within herself, and to develop her own perspective.

This brings us to the third lesson:

Maturity
=
Better Relationships

Meanwhile, as Psyche struggles to complete her tasks, Eros is searching for her. After undergoing a long healing process of his own, he sets out on a difficult journey to locate his lost partner. As Psyche is completing her final task, he finds her. In an act of exasperation, Eros appeals to Zeus, king of the gods, crying out that they have suffered enough. In reward for their bravery and love, Zeus makes Psyche immortal, and completes their reconciliation with Aphrodite. Soon Psyche and Eros bear a daughter whom they name Joy.

The view of love flowing from this story reveals that when the pursuit of love becomes a journey, it also becomes a promise for a more fulfilling life. Living into this promise can refine us and lead to a more complete and satisfying experience of life. The adventure often begins blindly with equal amounts of wonder and fear. It challenges the boundaries of common sense, and frequently thrusts us first into joy and then into the despair of disillusionment and failure. Thankfully, the power and presence of love can fill us with hope as we face the growthful tasks it has pushed us to confront. It is only when we are willing to grow that we are open to all of love's promise and potential. Otherwise, our view of love would be like looking through a tiny window and thinking that we have seen the entire landscape. Love provides the fuel for growing strength, patience, hope, and trust.

The fourth and final lesson stresses love's quality and nature:

Love is a Journey

The Group Responds

I pause after finishing the story and look around the room. The group is still absorbed in the story and appears thoughtful.

Bob begins our discussion by saying that he was annoyed at first when he heard the story came from a myth. "It made me feel like I was back in school. Then I realized this is really similar to what Trish and I are going through."

Trish agrees. "It's a relief to see that everyone faces a crisis in their relationship in different ways, and that our problems with our children can be a turning point in our relationship." She goes on to say how full of hope she was when she and Bob fell in love, and how determined she was to make her second marriage work. But—like Psyche, she realizes now—she's been afraid and has felt abandoned. Feeling like the ringmaster in their relationship is overwhelming her.

Karen could also see how the characters in the story represent parts of herself. "I know I'm like Eros. I don't want to have to reveal myself. That would mean I have to slow down and look at myself in the daylight."

"I agree with Trish," Cory says, glancing at Barry. "It's a relief to hear that all we've done is reach a turning point and that we haven't messed things up." She relates how she felt like everything started out so well, but after the children came, she and Barry lost that special spark of understanding that made them work as a couple.

Barry joins in, realizing that, in terms of the story line, having their children was like inviting in the ugly sisters; it had "spilled the oil," bringing their idyllic relationship into the light of day. Barry admits he gets touchy and angry and cuts Cory out, and doesn't even know why.

Everyone agrees that relationships start blissfully in the dark and then something happens. There is quiet for a moment as the group members think about their own lives. Then Trish says, "I also think we're trying to test the relationship. I think that sometimes when I complain, it is just my attempt to push Bob, to see how strong he is, how much he really cares about me."

Tom, quiet until now, admits, "Well, you're braver than I am. I feel this relationship is too good to be happening to me, especially after the mess my father made of his marriages. I'm afraid I will do something to alienate Cindy."

Cindy admits having the same fears, worrying that Tom might lose interest in her if she's too introverted. Tom looks at her reassuringly, and she smiles back.

Karen, with a hint of tears in her eyes, acknowledges that sometimes fear of pushing Leah away results in exactly that. She recounts a time when she was in a really foul mood, and Leah's feelings were hurt, just like Eros in the story. Leah left home and went out to a bar, leaving Karen afraid and furious.

Massimilla sums up what the group has been saying: Couples all tend to go through similar things; it is difficult to approach turning points in life; and it is frightening to think that by being ourselves, we may push away the people we love. But she says, "It helps to know it is going to happen and, when it does, we can make choices to help ourselves grow through it."

By this point, everyone is getting involved in the discussion. Michael jumps in and says that his relationship with Vanessa is still good, and that they love each other, but they have witnessed in their parents' relationships how love can get lost. He asks that the group discuss a little more about how "being yourself" can push someone away, and how to find your way back.

Trish opens up, saying that while falling in love was an unexpected gift for Bob and her after their former marriages, their divorces had left both of them feeling diminished, like failures. This feeling was compounded every time they had to deal with their exes or when a problem came up with one of the children. Then they seemed to become different people—wounded, angry, and discouraged. She admits, "That's why we're really here. We don't want to repeat the past. It hurts too much."

Relating back to the story, she continues. "The idea of Psyche's first task—sorting the seeds—really helps me to understand. It shows how carefully we have to sort things out and how overwhelming it feels at times. But if we keep trying, there is hope."

Vanessa, Michael's girlfriend and the youngest group member, speaks up. "I don't know about that. You're painting a grim, bleak future for us. Michael and I can't seem to decide whether or not to get married and the rest of you are talking about failure and divorces. God, why should we bother?"

Bob jumps in: "Don't forget Aphrodite—reconciliation. When Trish and I met, we really fell for each other." He goes on to say that when she got angry or pushed him, he didn't like it. He would be furious that she no longer seemed the sensuous, loving person he was so attracted to. "But," he says, with a smile, "the more I think about it now, the more I realize that person is still there somewhere and I've got to find her."

"That's a good point," Barry says. "We need to remember what's really important and not be afraid to look for what we've lost, instead of just sulking."

"Thank you," Trish replies. "It's good to hear that from a man."

Cindy adds that she feels that she gets so lost at times. "The pressure of trying to be supportive of Tom and doing everything else occasionally gets to be too much. I need for Tom to pursue me a little, maybe ask me for a 'date.'"

Remembering from the story that Eros was looking for Psyche, too, Tom responds, "I think we both may need to be looked for at times."

I remind the group that we also need some time apart to think, be with ourselves, and figure things out. Just as Eros and Psyche have to reclaim who they are in order to come back together in a stronger, more mature way. Unfortunately, most people that we see professionally did not know what happened when their relationships began to change. It frightened them, and so they started a power struggle in an attempt to force the other person to act the way they wanted them to, or the way they always had.

Leah realizes that this is what she was doing to Karen when she went out to the bar. "I was hurt, but now I realize I wanted to scare her good and make her be the way I wanted her to be."

"I totally agree!" Cory chimes in. "Before we got married, the minister told us that men go into a marriage wanting the relationship to never change, and women go in seeing the potentials they want it to live up to."

Several people groan in agreement.

This brings up something that frightens Vanessa. She saw her parents adjust to each other by hardening into roles of being a hardworking husband and pleasant wife. The roles looked good to outsiders, but she felt that their relationship was hollow. "They preferred their friends and jobs to each other. I don't think my dad would have even noticed if mom had found a lover and was gone several nights a week."

The laughter of a moment ago quickly dies away, and Michael, blue eyes blazing, speaks up. "Well, my dad would have noticed because there wouldn't have been anybody there for him to put down. My parents could look like Ozzie and Harriet, too, but underneath their facades, I think they were furious. Their relationship wasn't a journey. At best, it was a hostile truce."

The intensity in the room was palpable. Bob continues by telling us how he and his first wife began a power struggle soon after they married. They were trying to force each other to be the person they wished they had married. "She wanted me to be strong and supportive all of the time, with no needs of my own. I wanted her to like me, to admire how hard I worked, and how much I did for her." He paused, and then admitted feeling stupid because they had taken the same fight through twelve years of marriage and their divorce, in spite of the pain, struggle, and heartache.

I add that this happens to a lot of couples. They pull back from each other and would rather make a vain attempt to recapture the past or an ideal of relationship they refuse to give up, instead of facing reality and growing into the future.

This resonates with Trish, who shares that she was crushed when her first husband withdrew, and she gained fifteen pounds. "He started drinking and playing golf more and just seemed to ignore me and the children. I had married young and really looked up to him and took his criticism too seriously." She said that it took lot of therapy for her to get her spirit back, and to find the determination to build a better life. Until she sought help, she didn't realize that she had choices.

Massimilla takes this opportunity to restate the point that we all have choices. And that it is important to know more about how relationships work and the meaning of our problems if we are going to make healthier decisions.

Karen is skeptical and laments that it does not seem like there are that many choices in relationships; they either are going to grow, degenerate, or spin off into some kind of stalemate.

Trish responds to Karen's doubt by sharing what has helped her. "Remember that a relationship is a journey. I keep coming back to that. It reminds me that when we're off track, even if we are struggling, we can choose to grow."

I reflect that growth is always a choice.

Trish continues. "I also like the part about Psyche braving the underworld to complete her final task and reclaim her strength. I almost sold out my entire being trying to make the picture in my first marriage a pleasing one. That was a very dark period in my life."

When Bob says that he also sold himself short to try to make his first marriage work, Trish, surprised, asks, "Do men do that, too?"

"More than you know," Bob responds. "I was a pleaser from way back and didn't know it." He explained how it crept up on him slowly after he got married. He thought that if his wife were happy, everyone would be happy. Even though he worked long hours, he gradually began to do the laundry, fix meals, supervise homework, and go to all the school activities. His wife did more and more of what she wanted to do, joining clubs, charity activities and serving on various boards. "Looking back, I believe she was just trying to bolster her ego. But eventually, I crossed a bottom line, and something in me just snapped. Before I knew it, I'd sold out so much I couldn't recover and the relationship, for me, was dead."

The reality of turmoil is upsetting to Vanessa. She asks if she and Michael will have to go through this if they get married. Trish and Bob admit that they are facing similar struggles even now with each other.

Massimilla speaks directly to Vanessa's concerns by asking her to remember the rest of the story; facing problems can be a turning point, not a sign of failure. We need to learn how to grow throughout our lives, and being in a relationship can offer us a valuable opportunity to grow in ways not possible by ourselves.

I concur, and add that it is important to remember that love is growth.

This discussion brings up another question for Vanessa. She wants to know if the story is telling us that it is the woman's job to make the repairs when things go wrong.

Over a loud chorus of "no's!" Massimilla asks the group to look at the story within the story. It is important for each one of us to grow into a more mature capacity to love.

Taking my cue from confused looks on the men's faces, I add that it is a real challenge for a man in our culture to cultivate his strength *and* his capacity as a sensitive, responsive lover.

Trish, who is on a roll, says that while she finds the discussion hopeful and inspiring, she is afraid these helpful ideas are going to get lost the first time she and Bob clash over something.

Many nod in agreement. I acknowledge that this is a common fear, and a problem that we all will face. And, just like Psyche, we need help from several sources. Learning more about the craft of relating will help us turn the rough spots in our journey into opportunities that help us grow personally and come together as a couple. I also promise that we will talk about this more in our next meeting.

Others laugh when someone asks, "Do we have to wait until next week?"

This prompts a final question from Cindy. "If this story of Psyche and Eros is typical, how many times can it happen in our lives? It makes me think about how different Tom and I have turned out to be, and what different people we will be in twenty years from who we are today. Does this mean the story may repeat again in our lives?"

Massimilla tells her that it does, and that her question leads to an important thought on which to end the first session. The more fully we experience the story and grow from our crisis or bleak periods, the more confident we become in ourselves and in the durability of our relationship. At every turning point, our love has to evolve and we have to find ourselves again. Some examples of life-changing events are when children leave home; when we make career changes; when we experience spiritual growth, illnesses, or retirement. Or perhaps it is more accurate to say that the story will repeat itself in less disruptive or stressful ways if we remember the opportunities it offers—that a crisis is a turning point, that love equals growth, that growing brings maturity and better relationships, and that love is a journey full of promise. I believe that as we share our own stories, experiences, wisdom, and insights, you will see how these patterns have been repeated in your own lives many times. You, as the reader, may also think of some examples where it has happened in your lives without realizing it.

More Practical Applications

To help further illustrate some very practical applications for this story, and before we move to the nuts and bolts of how to apply the craft of relationship in your own life, we want to share examples of two different couples coming to a turning point, or crisis, at different phases in their relationship. And, how they have drawn insight and wisdom from the timeless myth of Eros and Psyche.

We counseled a couple who had been married for a few years. The husband was working long hours away from home, and thought everything was going well. He did not realize, in his absence, that his wife was beginning to feel like he no longer valued her. Out of her loneliness and resentment, she began to criticize him and complain that he didn't spend enough time with her. As she began to berate him for working so much, she crossed a boundary, and her husband no longer felt loved and admired the way he once had. He felt betrayed and burned and responded by withdrawing and spending even more time at work and playing racquetball with his friends. This left his wife feeling even more unloved and lonely. As soon as they heard Psyche's story and our explanation of it, they looked at each other. First they smiled. Then they laughed. The story had clicked with them and helped them see the pattern of disillusionment and separateness they were caught in and offered a way to find new hope.

In another situation, a couple had raised their children, and had finally moved into their dream home. At last, they thought they were ready to relax, enjoy the life they built, and to live happily together. Yet before long, they began arguing about little things, and these arguments escalated until they both felt misunderstood, unappreciated, and deeply perplexed.

Can you detect a recurring theme from our story as this couple faces a new stage in their lives? This new stage signals a need for their love to change and grow if they want to move to a deeper level of commitment and meaning in their relationship.

We all will experience these natural cycles of growth and change. However, such growth usually begins with dissatisfaction, which first requires that we have to let go of old ways, old ideals, and even some pleasures without holding onto resentment over what we have to give up. If we are alert and open to life, we will see that love wants to grow and enrich us in new and deeper ways during every stage of our lives. New beginnings, like births, are preceded by an uncomfortable period of time, arrive amidst pain and struggle, and yet bring with them the wonder and joy of new life.

PART TWO

THE CRAFT OF RELATIONSHIP

One hardly dares to say that love is the core of the relationship, though love is sought for and created in relationship; love is rather the marvel when it is there, but it is not always there, and to know another and to be known by another—that is everything.

—Florida Scott-Maxwell

3

INTIMATE COMMUNICATION:
THE CRAFT OF KNOWING EACH OTHER

The failure to register another's feelings is a major deficit in emotional intelligence, and a tragic failing in what it means to be human. For all rapport, the root of caring, stems from emotional attunement, from the capacity for empathy.

—Daniel Goldman

During the week between meetings, Massimilla and I thought about the new people who had joined us for this journey of four weeks. We remembered Bob, a large man with a shy, husky voice, and his wife, Trish, who was concerned about the practical aspects of a blended family. Both of them had suffered a lot in previous marriages. We noticed Tom's persona of assurance and Cindy's quiet apprehension about what would support their relationship after their children were out of the house, plus her fear of losing herself in Tom's active approach to life. We recalled Barry's comment about the honeymoon being over, an expression that we all could identify with in our own way. His wife, Cory, also had shared her feelings openly, admitting how much she disliked chaos and often felt driven to distraction by her children. Both of us had enjoyed Karen and Leah's lively presence. We understood how isolated they might feel in a culture that offered them no traditional support and how easily despair can overtake us when we feel outside of the mainstream. And we felt the fears that our youngest couple, Michael and Vanessa, had voiced as they shared their uncertainty about getting married were the same fears most of us have been haunted by.

The group now gathers for the second session. Everyone appears in good spirits and it almost feels like a reunion of old friends. We welcome each couple as they arrive, and invite them to get a cup of coffee or tea. It is evident from the easy rapport the group shares that we have developed enough confidence in each other to support our discussion of today's topic: intimate communication.

To set the stage, I begin by sharing that deep inside, most of us have a longing for intimacy. A desire to share ourselves with another person, feel accepted and understood, and to be able to return this gift to our partner. No matter how wounded or cynical we may become, we still know in our hearts that we need each other. On the most basic level, we need each other in order to survive. We also need each other in order to experience the vitality and inner security that intimacy can bring. The kind of security that assures us we can count on each other through both joyful and stormy times. It is the security that we will discover each other anew as we grow. The craft of intimacy promises that we will continue growing in our relationships, and even when love seems lost, we have the potential to discover it again, and re-create it on a deeper level.

I continue by pointing out that most of us have heard that communication is the key to a good relationship. And, most of us have learned that intimate communication is not as easy as it sounds. It can often run aground on the shoals of our vulnerabilities, past insults and hurts, and unrealistic expectations. Our lessons in the craft of relationship are going to give us the skills and insights to navigate these rough waters. There may be tension between us and we do not know what to do to make things better. Or we may find ourselves frustrated if we think we are not being listened to, really listened to, both heard *and* understood. Becoming skilled at understanding each other can bring down the walls of resentment and isolation. Learning and practicing the skills we will introduce next will build trust, open our hearts, and inspire us to give and receive love and support.

Golden Rules of Intimate Relationships

Intimacy requires a special kind of communication. A style of communication based on what we consider the golden rules of relationship; golden because following them will create deeper intimacy and greater happiness. Our rules are based on value, respect, kindness, and trust. We pay attention to the things we value. If we value our relationship, we learn that the time, effort, and emotions we put into it are acts of love. We need to remember that if we love someone, we must treat him or her with respect. Listening carefully and being patient are signs of respect and kindness. Intimate communication requires that we share our deepest selves with our partner. In order to feel free to share ourselves—our feelings, thoughts, dreams, hurts, resentments, and joys—we first must have trust. Attention, kindness, and respect are the foundation of trust. Trust makes sharing easier, more comfortable, and more satisfying. We feel safe because we know our partner loves us, listens patiently, and takes us seriously rather than becoming hostile and critical when we share our deepest thoughts, feelings, fears, and dreams.

The first steps toward successful intimate communication are usually the hardest because we have learned to hide our vulnerabilities and deep feelings. To help make the learning process easier, we will describe the necessary ground work and then offer some guidelines that support our craft such as timing, preparation, openness, seeking to understand, being willing to learn, being willing to respond, and being willing to change. We will also explore situations where, in the heat of the moment, we may feel so blocked by hurt and anger that we arc in danger of forgetting how much we love our partner. When we find ourselves in a similar situation, we must stop and explore our feelings alone until we understand what is driving us. Only then can we shift our mood and back away from blaming either our partner or ourselves.

At this point I introduce a contemporary story about two different couples. Even though the couples in the story are fictional characters, they strongly represent aspects of those we have counseled, and their experiences will resonate with *anyone* who has been in a committed relationship. We will take periodic breaks from the story to discuss our thoughts, feelings, and reactions.

A Contemporary Story

Steve and Ann married when he was 28 and she was 25. During their early years, they were friends as well as lovers. Marriage had helped Steve settle into his career and he had worked hard. Ann taught school until their two children were born. *Once both children reached school age, she recertified as a reading teacher and currently works part-time. Now in his early 40s, Steve thinks they have done well yet at times, finds himself angry with Ann for no apparent reason. When he realizes that he is becoming hurtfully sarcastic toward her, he becomes confused and sees that telling himself everything is fine no longer works. Ann has not changed. She is not saying or doing anything she has not always done. Steve wonders why he is suddenly so angry, so critical of her.*

Steve is also surprised and distressed when he notices a powerful attraction to a woman at work. He figures out that the attraction is not just about sex; she listens to what he says and compliments him. It embarrasses Steve to admit that he wants Ann to listen to him more, to be interested in things he likes, and to respect his opinion. Plus, he wants to be able to share his frustrations about his job and their finances, and his dreams of traveling more, or starting his own consulting firm with Ann without her getting upset, defensive, or being too tired to pay attention. He also realizes that a little more physical passion between them would not hurt. He cannot remember the last time he felt like Ann really wanted to make love with him. The more he thinks about his situation, the lonelier and more discouraged he feels.

Steve wonders if he is hoping for too much from his relationship. At the same time he is getting more scared of Ann's imagined reactions and wonders what would actually happen if he shares how he is feeling with her. He is also worried because a friend told him that a counselor had said that in order to have a good relationship, you have to work on it every day. That does not sound encouraging or like very much fun. Just more work and worry.

A few weeks later, Steve and Ann attended a wedding for Steve's nephew. Lasting the entire weekend, the event turns out to be a large family reunion. On several occasions Steve finds himself seated next to one of his favorite cousins, Maggie, who he has not seen in years. Ten years older than Steve, Maggie had been his regular baby-sitter when he was a child. Over the years, through the family grapevine, Steve remembered hearing that Maggie had gone through some hard times in her marriage. She and her husband, Jim, had even separated for several months before deciding to reconcile. Yet, throughout the weekend, both Steve and Ann notice how much Maggie and Jim seem to enjoy each other.

A few days later, Steve decides to phone Maggie and invite her to lunch. He trusts her and feels she may have learned some things from her experiences that would be helpful for he and Ann. Perhaps he might better understand his vague, troubling dissatisfaction and articulate what it was he is looking for, even though he is not completely sure himself.

* * *

After greeting each other and ordering lunch, Steve hesitantly shares his uneasy feeling that something is wrong with his relationship. Maggie listens intently and then confides, "Jim and I ignored our disturbing feelings and let things go too far. It sounds like you may be noticing them early, before you get too angry, or Ann gets too hurt and angry back. We married young and had to struggle a lot as we tried to grow up emotionally. But we loved each other and that gave us the strength, or maybe the stubbornness, not to let go too easily. We had some hard times, though."

"It sounds like you and Jim must have learned some answers. So are the advice columns right, is communication really the key to a good relationship?" Jim asked.

Maggie replies that she does not think it is that simple. She had tried talking with Jim years before. She remembers being happy at first because he would always listen, which was more than many of her friends' husbands would do. "But when I was unhappy with our life, or hurt by something he had done, he never said much back. He just tried to cheer me up or make me happy." Maggie admits that she began to wonder if he really heard what she was saying; if he sincerely was trying to understand how she felt. "The more I talked, the madder I got. At the same time, I felt belittled and isolated." She sighs as she remembers their hard times, and then continues. "Eventually, Jim became overwhelmed by my feelings, got mad back, and yelled that nothing ever made me happy. Before long, our relationship was gridlocked. Both of us were angry."

Maggie goes on to share that when Jim and she started counseling, they learned about stagnant periods, and that conflicts and even crises in a relationship can be turning points. "In our case, the issues began with me feeling misunderstood and demeaned, but they can be about anything: sex, money, children, who earns the most, who spends the most, even old patterns we need to let go of so we can learn a new way of living together." She also remembers that the counselor pointed out that intimacy is the core of a relationship, and that the first step in dealing with a relationship problem is to realize that intimate communication is different from ordinary communication. Jim soon learned that making her happy was not his job; trying to understand each other is much more important.

Steve reflects that what Maggie is saying makes perfect sense.

"We felt the same way, but this was all new to Jim and me," Maggie continues, saying that since it was all new, they had no idea how to start. "Obviously what we had been doing wasn't working, so we had to learn what to do." Maggie then shares a metaphor that she and Jim find very valuable and still use.

"Our counselor told us that intimate communication is like taking a ball, like a volleyball or beach ball, and playing catch," Maggie begins. "In a good game of catch both people are energized and have to pay attention to the ball as it is thrown back and forth. People need each other to play catch. One person can't play very well alone."

Steve admits that while it makes sense, it sounds a bit simplistic.

"Yes, until you begin to understand all that it represents," Maggie responds. "If you're going to live intimately, you have to learn how to play catch every day. The ball represents all of the things in life you share with your partner. 'Tossing' and 'catching' are the methods of communication that we use. In order to be a good ballplayer, you have to take the time to learn how to throw the ball in a way that makes it easier for your partner to catch. And, you have to be paying attention in order to catch the ball being tossed to you. Just like we have to learn how to give time and attention to our relationship in the midst of our busy lives. Attention is the surest sign of being valued. And, it becomes an important part of the bridge that joins us in love and makes intimate communication possible."

We pause to highlight the first golden rule: Attention in a relationship is equal to being valued. Giving attention to our partner is the most fundamental way of saying, "I love you, I care about what you say, and I value you and your opinions."

$$Attention = Value$$

When Steve ventures to say that warmth and caring are also important, Maggie replies that they are helpful but we do not always feel warm and caring. "Jim and I had to learn that intimacy is not defined by how we feel, but how we treat each other. For example, it is easy to be kind to Jim when he agrees with me, and tempting to withhold kindness when I am unhappy. But it is critically important that we learn how to use respect and kindness even when we disagree or are angry. Intimacy is valuable and worth protecting," Maggie explains. "Believe me, when I don't feel loved, or am treated badly, I lose trust fast."

Maggie also shares that her counselor reminded them that many of us have very distinct personalities and often see things differently. The beauty of intimacy is that we are not trying to make others the same, or insist that they agree with us. Respect and kindness help form the foundation of intimacy. When we are patient with each other it shows kindness, and when we listen carefully we convey respect.

I pause at this point in the story to point out our second and third golden rules in relationship: careful listening is a sign of respect, and patience toward our partner is a sign of kindness.

Listening = Respect
Patience = Kindness

Steve is puzzled because he has always believed that a happy relationship meant being in harmony with Ann. "But we need to agree somewhere, have something in common, don't we?" Steve questions, still looking a little confused.

Maggie quickly agrees and uses the ball analogy to further explain. "Once Jim and I got pretty good at playing catch with simple thoughts and feelings, we slowly began to toss and catch more complex things, such as our values, hopes, and ideals."

She goes on to confide that the first thing Jim and she agreed on was that they wanted their relationship to feel important and alive. Yet talking about the things they treasure, like how wonderful it felt when they fell in love, and even the early dreams they lost, was a mixture of reaffirmation and sadness.

At first they found it difficult to discuss new dreams. They did not want to be disappointed again. "But soon it became exciting. It really energized how we live together," Maggie finishes with a big smile and sigh.

While Steve really enjoys the hope and enthusiasm he hears in Maggie's voice, he remains focused on the ways in which Ann and he are different. "But Ann and I call a lot of our own shots. We tend to avoid areas where we disagree. Our concerns are more down-to-earth and mundane than dreams. We've never agreed on how often to make love, for instance, and we acquiesce to each other on a lot of things, like how to deal with holidays and in-laws. I'm not sure I want to rock the boat. It could get pretty intense."

Maggie quickly assures him that it could, and will, get intense. But she hastens to add the positive side to the stresses change brings. Having worked out shared values allows her to be herself because she does not feel like she has simply given in. "When I do give in it's not to create a false sense of harmony, but because I've decided that it is the best thing to do," she affirms. She then adds that this honest and open approach has helped her keep from doing things that might make Jim feel betrayed or uneasy.

Steve looks a little overwhelmed by what Maggie is saying. After a quiet moment he says, "It sounds like trying to become more intimate could be dangerous. What if we find out we don't have shared values? At the very least, what you're saying sounds like a lot of hard work."

Maggie assures Steve that he has an important choice to make. If he wants to revitalize his life with Ann, it is a lot easier to choose to do it now. And she bets that if he feels dissatisfied then Ann must, too, on some level. "The longer you wait, the better the chance your relationship will become more hurtful." She confesses that Jim and she were separated for six months, and that it was painful. She learned the hard way what she is talking about.

Maggie touches Jim's arm and continues. "But even the pain of separation was worth what we gained. Underneath all of our turmoil, Jim and I both wanted the other person to hold us, to take care of us, to understand our pain and joy. We wanted to be nurtured, to feel excitement together, to feel like we were important to each other."

Maggie ends this part of the conversation by telling Steve that, sadly, the foundation of trust and respect they once had was lost. They had to back off until they could regain it. That is why they separated. She looks pointedly at

Steve and says, "It was a bitter disappointment for both of us to do that. Physically living apart seemed to symbolize failure and could have been the first step in breaking up permanently. It could easily have gone that way. This is part of the danger you mentioned a few moments ago. When we first met, Jim and I felt like we could talk about anything. We told each other everything about our lives. We thought we were each other's best friend."

She reassures Steve that, through work, love, and time, she and Jim have regained the feelings they feared were lost forever.

I begin our discussion by asking the group if they could see a connection between the couples in this story, and Eros and Psyche. I am sure that most of them picked up on the fact that Maggie and Jim had gotten stuck at a turning point in their journey, as have Steve and Ann. I ask the group to recall the moment when Psyche spilled the hot oil and burned Eros. From that point on Eros and Psyche had to learn how to reclaim themselves, and then how to relate to each other more maturely if they were to renew the foundation of intimacy that supported them.

Massimilla adds that many of us have experienced the same sort of burning. Generally, it causes us to quit talking to each other because we feel like we cannot agree on anything. When we try to talk we may feel like we are actually making things worse. Then we may try to act like everything is fine and ignore the need to discuss anything. But this approach leaves us feeling even more lonely, trapped, and resentful. Soon isolation breeds suspicion and erodes the goodwill we once had. She also shares that she has seen couples so angry that, to borrow Maggie's metaphor, their communication looked as though they were throwing the ball at each other's head. This stage continues to get worse and worse, more hopeless, and more furious.

Before we return to Maggie and Steve, I share a story about a couple who were on the threshold of giving up on their relationship. Before taking the final step, they made a decision to attend our seminar. During the first meeting they shared that they—like most of us—had started out loving each other. But after eleven years of increasing frustration, they lost their passion and were about to give up. They were amazed by the story of Eros and Psyche and learned that conflicts are meant to be turning points, rather than an end, in love's journey. They were surprised to discover that differences are not only normal, they are the exact seeds we need in order to grow a more complete version of love. And they were comforted to find out that other couples were experiencing this same pattern. After diligently applying the skills we cover in this seminar, they were able to begin to rekindle their feelings of respect, kindness, trust, and appreciation for each other's uniqueness. Soon, they began to fall in love again.

Steve says that he likes the idea of a game of catch, that it is something to which he can easily relate. He asks Maggie to review the rules of this intimacy building game.

Maggie is happy to; she loves what this practice has done for her relationship. She begins by reminding Steve that we have to learn how to throw the ball so that our partner can easily catch and toss it back. The first toss has to be gentle enough to handle. If we throw too hard or too wild, the other person is going to get frustrated and angry and either stop playing, or throw it back to us the same way. "I used to badger Jim about drinking too much on the weekend. I told him it was disgusting. I didn't find him attractive and I was worried about his health. Of course these comments made him feel guilty and attacked. Then he would get angry and withdraw. When I learned to be honest about how it made me feel, everything changed. Simple, direct honesty about feelings was a toss Jim could easily catch."

Steve motions that he wants to hear more, so Maggie shares what their counselor taught her to say. "Jim, when you drink on the weekends, I feel insulted and a little scared. I feel like you are unhappy and afraid to talk to me about what's really bothering you." Maggie admits that Jim still got angry, but then he began to listen to her and to think about what she had said.

This memory causes Maggie to sit back in her seat and reflect. Then she blurts, "He really knew how to upset me. He would say, 'You always mess up your checkbook.' Or, 'You never remember to pick up my things at the cleaners.' The words 'always' and 'never' sound incredibly judgmental to me. As you might guess, my return ball toss always came back at his head."

Steve understands Maggie's point. It startles him to see how much easier it seems to blame his wife than to figure out how he really feels. These thoughts prompt him to ask Maggie if sharing her feelings ever makes her feel more vulnerable. She replies that at first it did. But after a while she found that sharing herself showed trust.

Golden rule #4: Sharing ourselves shows trust. I emphasize that withholding what we think and feel makes our partners feel belittled, alienated, and resentful.

Sharing Yourself
=
Trust

Steve tells Maggie that he never connected sharing himself with trust, and she explains how, when Jim heard how she felt about his drinking and how important their relationship was to her, he listened. Even though it made him angry at first. This helped her begin to trust him again.

"Ann and I seem to get into things at the wrong time. How critical is timing in these discussions?" Steve asks. He is impressed by how much Maggie is telling him. She responds that it is important if we are honestly concerned and not trying to be manipulative. She returns to the ball analogy to elaborate. "If I have an idea or problem and want to talk about it, it's like having the ball in my hand ready to play catch. But unless the topic is urgent, one of us may not want to play catch at certain times. I'm pretty wiped out when I first get home from work, and Jim's asleep by eleven." Smiling now at the memory, she shares that they figured out that when one of them feels compelled to talk when the other one is not responsive, it usually means they are excited about something, they have slipped up, or they have let themselves get too busy and have ignored each other, and one of them feels left out.

After digesting this perspective, Steve acknowledges that it really upsets him when Ann hits him with a load of problems as soon as he gets home from work, just when he needs a chance to relax and change gears. And, to further complicate matters, he admits that talking about problems has never been easy for them. "I know Ann gets upset when she thinks I'm lecturing her. I can even feel myself slipping into my father's voice when we talk about our budget, or buying something new for the house."

Maggie points out, to reassure Steve that he is not alone in his challenges, that their counselor told them that lecturing is a pretty common problem on both sides. And that lecturing is not playing catch; it is one person throwing ball after ball at the other person. "If Jim does that I feel attacked and resentful. As soon as it starts I usually put up a wall and the balls simply bounce off. But I do it, too. I've heard myself sound like my mother, and while it catches his attention, that tone of voice makes me shudder. She was always a great one for making pronouncements, sounding like the ultimate, I-know-everything authority." Maggie notes that she remembers during her childhood that her mother's pronouncements caused her to think that what she had to say did not matter. "She made me feel stupid—and so I shut her out."

Maggie's honest reflections allow Steve to be honest, too. He wonders out loud if the behavior is genetic; her mother sounds like his father, laying down the law.

Maggie has more to say about timing. "Then there were the times when Jim and I would both come together with an agenda to discuss. We both had a ball to toss," Maggie begins, "which isn't any easier. Jim would throw his and, instead of catching it and throwing it back, I would ignore his and throw mine. That's a good strategy for cutting someone off, but power plays like that ruin intimacy." Maggie wants Steve to think of it this way: if partners are really listening, they have to put their own agenda on hold. Someone has to be willing to put their ball down and be open to receive their partner's toss. They have to concentrate on listening completely and then responding to each point until they have worked their way through the particular topic or problem. Then they can begin another game. Being carefully listened to and honestly, but respectfully, answered seems to change both people, whether or not they agree. They feel closer and more real.

Maggie is pleased to see that Steve is still interested. "Whew!" he exclaims. When Steve says that it seems like something they will have to work on every day, Maggie responds that it is work at first, like learning to ride a bicycle. "You have to pay close attention until you get the hang of it. Then it becomes fun, even though we all face some steep hills at times. For me, intimacy with Jim brings a quiet kind of joy to every day. If we fail to connect during a day, I miss it."

Steve thanks Maggie sincerely but adds that he had no idea she knew so much about relationships or was so intuitive. He also muses that everything they have discussed seems difficult and challenging, but also exciting, provoking him to think in ways he has never thought before.

In response to his appreciation, Maggie offers one more piece of advice. She tells Steve that she can tell he likes to think problems through carefully and then talk about them, and that he has been letting them marinate for a long time. But he needs to be careful. Ann may be a lot more open than he is. "She may like to talk questions over as a help to thinking them through. If you don't share what you're thinking about with her, when you finally bring all of this up, she is going to feel ambushed. You will scare her, make her angry, and she will feel left out."

Steve looks confused in response to this, so Maggie adds, "Haven't you heard that opposites attract? Or realize that you and Ann very likely approach problems differently? Anyway, just please take my advice and talk to her!"

After Maggie leaves, Steve takes out a pencil and a small pad he uses for work and begins to jot down some notes. At the end of his notes he writes:

Attention Shows Value

Listening Shows Respect

Patience Shows Kindness

Sharing Ourselves Shows Trust

Judging from the looks of interest in the group, I can tell it is time to begin our discussion. Before I am able to say anything, Karen speaks up and asks us to add the list of guidelines to the list of golden rules for intimate communication that Massimilla has written on the board. She also shares with the group what matters most to her. "For me, attention, respect, kindness, and trust are fundamental."

I like what she has chosen to highlight, so to begin to flush out the list of guidelines, I ask the rest of the group what impresses them as the first thing that is important in intimate communication.

Tom volunteers timing. "Timing has a lot to do with whether Cindy or I can be receptive. I agree with the story. I think right after work is a bad time. When you're getting ready for work isn't so great either." Several in the group nod in agreement, so *timing* becomes the first guideline we write on the board.

Bob suggests preparation. "I need to think for a minute, clear my head, or I am afraid that my first toss of the ball could be really wild." Others agree.

Preparation becomes our second guideline.

Cindy admits that, for her, the toughest one is putting her agenda on hold in order to listen. Cory agrees, and adds, "Putting my agenda on hold *and* my resentments. My parents used to drive me crazy. Every argument they had they would bring out a laundry list of resentments that went back decades."

Bob joins in and says that he has done the same thing in his former marriage. They would go all the way back to when they were dating for their list. He confesses that the lingering resentment was really hurtful and useless.

When Barry wonders where listening fits into all this, Leah responds that while she thinks listening is important, the attitude we listen with must come first. "We need to listen in a real effort to understand each other. We have to listen until we understand how the other person feels." Several people raise their voice in agreement.

There is a reflective pause, and then Trish speaks up with her thoughts. "It seems like we have to listen until we understand what it's like to be in the other person's shoes. My first husband and I briefly tried counseling and he would say, 'I just can't understand Patricia at all. She won't listen to me.' Then the therapist said, 'I thought that in order to understand Patricia, you need to listen to her.'" Sadly, Trish says that he never did catch on. He always thought she was thinking what he believed she was thinking.

"Nothing is more frustrating than feeling misunderstood by someone you love," Cindy adds. Karen asks if *seeking to understand* should be the next guideline

I affirm that this is the next guideline, and that this has become a popular term for people who teach communication skills. We add *seeking to understand* to our list.

"I was impressed by Steve's willingness to learn from Maggie," Tom remarks. "Don't you think the willingness to learn from each other is important, too?"

His comment is met with a small chorus of approval.

Karen, accurately summing up what we have discussed, articulates that both sides should be seeking to understand each other, and willing to learn from each other.

There is another chorus of agreement.

The room becomes quiet as I wait to see what else our perceptive participants will come up with. Vanessa is the first to break the silence by asking why I wrote, "be willing to learn" instead of, "learn from each other."

Good observation. I respond by telling her that while I agree, I do not think it is complete. Massimilla joins in and captures everyone's attention with her insight that she thinks both sides have to be willing to change. And that truly understanding the other person changes us. Even if we do not agree with them, we usually move from being defensive to sympathetic, and this means we have grown. We are emotionally attuned with each other whether or not we agree. "We've deepened our relationship and feel good about each other, even if we do not agree."

I add *be willing to change* to our list and ask the group if they can think of anything else.

Barry pipes up that while he thinks listening has been covered under the golden rules, he still believes that we have to listen and say something back that shows we understand what the other person is feeling. "At work we call it active listening. For example, If I come home and Cory tells me she is really upset because the children would not take their naps, I might reply, 'It sounds like you are very frustrated or disappointed you didn't get some things done that you wanted to.'"

Massimilla agrees that this is a good point. "In addition to showing Cory you understand how she's feeling, you have also given her a chance to talk more and clarify her feelings rather than getting stuck in an angry mood that could turn sour. Listening carefully and then responding by giving a summary of the feelings you've heard can be very helpful."

I share with the group that the hard part about responding in this manner is overcoming the feeling that in some way we are acting, or manipulating the other person. We tend to think that how we relate should be natural and spontaneous. But in reality it is a skill we have to practice until it becomes natural and spontaneous.

Leah expresses that she has heard of active listening, too, but thinks it is just as important for Karen to understand how she is thinking as it is to understand how she is feeling.

Massimilla concurs and tells the group that we will talk more about that next week. She also mentions that we have to understand or help each other clarify how we are thinking, as well as how we are feeling.

Cory counters that while she agrees, she has to be very careful. "I tend to give advice and lecture Barry, or try to make him feel better before I really understand what he's trying to say."

Michael agrees, too, but says that he does not think we come by these skills naturally. We have to learn them and then practice.

I add *be willing to respond* to our list, and then acknowledge the group for coming up with a strong list of guidelines for intimate communication.

Timing

Preparation

Seeking to Understand

Being Willing to Learn

Being Willing to Respond

Being Willing to Change

After a short break, we continue our discussion. "It felt so good to hear that you can disagree with your partner and still be emotionally attuned. I've always tended to think disagreement means you are mismatched," Vanessa offers.

"Me, too," Michael responds, and then to make sure he understands the concept, says, "I need to listen carefully and respond until I understand how Vanessa feels. This means I have to put aside whether I think she's right, is asking the wrong question, is being logical, critical, or whatever, until later."

Massimilla tells him that he is on track, and then offers another example of how listening carefully and responding can become more creative. "Suppose Barry comes home and starts complaining about what a mess the house is in. Cory might say, 'It sounds like you are angry at me.' Then Barry might reply, 'No, I'm not really angry with you. I just had a lot of problems at the office today.' In this situation, a potentially serious misunderstanding has been avoided. Cory has shown that she's heard him, is trying to understand how he is feeling. Her effort helps him articulate what is really going on."

I affirm this positive approach and then elaborate on what a scenario might look like without really seeking to understand. "Barry could have come home and told Cory, 'I've worked hard all day and don't want to hear about more problems.' Or in the second case, Cory could have said back to him, 'If you think keeping a house with two small children is so easy why don't you try it.' Both of these answers can create negative feelings."

This makes sense to Trish, who adds that she needs to feel she can share things safely with Bob and trust he will try to understand and value her. "For instance, when we were looking for a new house a few months ago, we went into one that I said just didn't feel right. When I said this, Bob got a little huffy and tried to sell me on all its economic advantages: the good price, resale potential, location, and so on." She admits that his reaction made her feel stupid. Bob responds that he was just trying to make a rational decision and that now, looking back, and hearing how his remarks made Trish feel, he is sorry he handled it that way.

Vanessa is struck by how easily we can misunderstand each other, but thinks the analogy of tossing the ball respectfully, patiently, and lovingly could really help them avoid similar problems. Michael enthusiastically agrees and says that the mental picture of playing verbal catch will help him keep his perspective. "I hope keeping my focus on gentle tosses and being willing to receive Vanessa's throws will make it easier for us to make good decisions."

This seems like a good time to shift gears and focus on some additional specifics we have encountered in our two sessions together. I ask the group if anything stuck out for them, either in the stories, or in the group discussion.

Cory immediately responds that she was really glad to hear Maggie say that we should not have to work on our relationship every day. Barry suggests that it actually sounds more like they need to work on themselves. "It is daunting to try to remember all of those things: to pay attention, to be kind, respectful, listen, understand, learn, *and* be willing to change. Learning about them will certainly make me think more about what I am doing."

Leah jumps in and says that she believes there is a difference between being active, interested, and loving, and "working" on something. *Working on* seems too dry, like something you get paid to do. She pauses, and then notes that she liked Maggie's idea that a good relationship should bring a quiet sense of joy to each day.

This resonates with Trish. "I think the joy comes from feeling valued and understood. Not agreed with, placated, or handled."

Bob confesses that he has always been afraid that if Trish is not happy, she might leave.

Trish really understands that, but adds that it is not that simple, that it goes deeper than just being happy. "For me the real deep unhappiness comes from not being honored, listened to, and valued."

Bob feels the same way. He adds that when he used to talk to his ex-wife about his hopes, dreams, or fears, she would get agitated. "If I was upset, she told me just to quit my job, follow my dream, and be happy. But that wasn't the point. She wanted me to feel like she was being supportive, but really, she just wanted me to stop bothering her. That left me feeling cut off, confused, and even childish."

I need to underscore the important point being made. "Many times, we have to listen to help our partner evolve to the place when they can articulate or recognize what they are really struggling with. Only then should we add our thoughts, feelings, and reactions."

Placating sentiments really irk Cory, who laments that she hates it when someone says to her, 'I just want you to be happy.' She once dated a man who said that all the time and that it only served to put up a brick wall between them. She shakes her head at the memory. "The surprising thing was, he appeared totally shocked when I said I didn't feel cared for or loved. He said he thought about me all the time."

Vanessa states strongly that simply saying that you think about someone all the time does not equal real love. She feels that you have to say it *and* show it. You have to make contact. "I treasure the contact Michael makes. He calls when he is away on trips, talks with me in the evening about little things, and treats our weekend shopping as a time to have fun together, rather than as a time simply to do chores. I guess that is 'attention,' too."

The group seems to relax into a comfortable silence as people reflect on their own experiences of giving and receiving quality time and attention.

Tom has a question about respect and kindness and wants to go back to the golden rules for a minute. He likes clarity and knowing what is expected of him. "I've seen a lot of relationships, especially in my parents' generation, that seem to have plenty of respect and kindness, but not that much closeness."

Several heads nod in agreement so we know this is important to the group. I respond by saying that I think it is easy to confuse polite behavior with a deeper form of respect and kindness. In intimate relationships kindness is more than simple etiquette. It calls for valuing the needs and wants of the other person and showing that you value them by the way you speak and act.

Tom asks for examples, so I share that I think I am being polite when I open the door for Massimilla. If I have an armful of books and she opens the door for me, that is kindness. In our relationship, being on time with each other is polite and kind. Calling each other when we will be late so the other person will not worry is an act of kindness.

Massimilla takes the examples to a deeper level. "In lovemaking, for example, polite behavior may be nice or irrelevant. But kindness toward our lover, and understanding and valuing the feelings and desires of each other, are essential."

In response, Tom ventures, "So it's easy to put on a polite front, but that doesn't mean you are close. Am I right?"

Cindy, playfully slapping his leg, insists, "It doesn't even mean you're friends."

Vanessa wants to know how you can be respectful if you are being misunderstood. "It seems like the minute I open my mouth, Michael thinks I'm criticizing, and retaliates."

Cory jumps in. "Barry's favorite response to me is that he can't get anything right. As though I were attacking him."

I ask the group if they have any suggestions.

Michael replies that it sounds like he needs to listen to everything Vanessa has to say *before* he decides whether or not he is being criticized.

When Tom asks, "Is this a guy thing?" several women immediately answer, "Oh, no!"

Cindy is quick to add, "But I think when you say, 'I can't get anything right,' it may be a little boy thing. It sounds sulky or childish."

Tom grins and says, "Ouch!"

Massimilla points out that deciding how you feel before you have listened carefully will put up another wall. It is a refusal to play ball, even though you really need to say, 'I am feeling defensive and want to start this game over.'

Leah wants to know what to do when she is angry or resentful, or when the first toss hits one of her hot buttons, whether or not it was meant to.

"You can count to ten before you answer, just like our mothers told us to," Trish says, laughing. "It works for me."

Tom interjects that he thinks it would be important to say 'let's stop and start over.' And if we are really angry, we might need a day or two to cool off first.

That seems too long to wait for Trish, who says, "I'm afraid our problem would be forgotten or buried, and cause even more resentment and anger in the future."

Karen suggests that they could set up a definite time to try the discussion again, but wants to know if there is anything helpful they can do while they are cooling off to help better understand what happened.

Massimilla responds to this. She points out that she looks at our hot buttons, or tender spots, as signals we need to pay attention to. She suggests, as a first step, to write everything we can think of about them in a journal. Ask ourselves why we are feeling defensive or aggressive and write about that. Ask ourselves who is really saying what we heard that upset us. Is it a voice from the past, perhaps from our father, mother, or some teacher, that makes us feel criticized, belittled, stupid, or whatever we may feel? Usually, we will get an insight within a paragraph or two. She then gives an example of a time when Bud was really busy and she was feeling lonely. She began writing and soon discovered how powerless she had felt as a child competing for her father's attention.

I added that I do the same thing. "I write down how I feel and everything that comes to mind without trying to censor it, or figure anything out. It usually doesn't take long until an insight is revealed that shifts my mood, or helps me understand what I'm feeling. I remember one Saturday when I was taking it easy and Massimilla asked me if I had any plans. In a flash, my relaxed mood snapped and her innocent comment became a call to battle stations. As I started writing about my feelings, an image of my grandmother came to me. I realized how controlling she was and how much I resented some of the things she said to me. Things like, 'quit sitting there and get busy.' The kind of admonitions I have to be careful not to say to myself."

Michael exclaims that he can totally relate. "Sometimes, when Vanessa says something to me, I think I hear my mother, grandmother, and a long line of teachers telling me how I haven't measured up." He wonders why he has not realized what was going on sooner.

I encourage him to not be hard on himself. We always have more to learn about our feelings. When we are young we are taught to control them. Too often that means we are taught to deny them. That sets us up to have them bounce back on us later.

Massimilla, continuing this train of thought, adds that when a tender area where we have been made to feel hurt, vulnerable, or belittled, is touched, our anger, sadness, or hostility that has been stored for years may rush up and take us over, possess us, before we know it, and we seem to lose ourselves.

Tom wants to know when he says, "I'm being driven crazy," where in him that is coming from. He says that if he can figure that out, then he can do something about it. And that it will make it easier for him to 'play catch' with Cindy.

Massimilla assures him that developing the capacity to be intimate forces us to get to know ourselves pretty well.

Karen groans that this means more work, and the rest of us laugh.

I agree with Trish when she concludes that the idea is to stay calm, know what we feel, but refuse to let hurts from old wounds take over.

Before we leave, Vanessa says that she would like to add one more thing about Michael. "One of the things I like best about him is his ability to laugh at himself. After we've had an argument, he can be pretty humorous about how we acted. Just knowing that makes me feel safe."

In closing, I remind the group to keep in mind that it is difficult to learn everything we need to know about the craft of intimate communication in a short time. We have covered a lot of ground today. We have talked about the golden rules that support a loving relationship, the guidelines for intimate communication, and how best to shift our moods by exploring our feelings to find out what is really upsetting us. Next week, when we talk about how opposites attract and later collide, we will really be continuing the same subject.

Tools for the craft of intimate relationships

Essential Lessons and Foundation Stones:

Crisis = Turning Point

Love = Growth

Maturity = Better Relationships

Love is a journey

Golden Rules:

Attention	=	Value
Patience	=	Kindness
Listening	=	Respect
Sharing Yourself	=	Trust

Guidelines:

- Timing
- Preparation
- Seeking to Understand
- Being Willing to Learn
- Being Willing to Respond
- Being Willing to Change

4

UNDERSTANDING AND APPRECIATION: THE CRAFT OF BEING UNIQUE AND TOGETHER

The opposite is beneficial; from things that differ comes the fairest attunement; all things are born through strife.

—Heraclitis

Our third meeting takes place on a gray Saturday morning. People are arriving after walking briskly through a spring rain. Soon, with coffee and tea cups filled, the group is ready to begin.

Almost immediately Cindy announces enthusiastically that she and Tom have been waiting all week to hear what is going to be said about opposites. She goes on to explain that it seems like many of their problems come from the fact that they are living life together with different scripts. Amid laughter, someone remarks that they are not the only ones to feel this way.

Still smiling, I accentuate our theme for the day:

*Love always seeks
to understand the individual*

Pulling from our collective experience and observations, I offer some of the foundational thoughts that led to this theme. When we first are attracted to someone, we revel in our differences. Doing things together, as well as sharing our diverse experiences, is delightful. During this time, we devote hours to learning about each other, exploring how we have dealt with life in different ways, and admiring each other's strengths and preferences. We are intrigued with how our needs differ and the ways we have sought to satisfy them.

The first bloom of love and our interest in our lover may carry us through months, or even years, of love and harmony. Yet inevitably, the pressures of our everyday lives intrude, and we begin to forget how much we treasured our partner's uniqueness, which was initially defined by the way he or she was different from us. It is our uniqueness that makes the relationship vital and dynamic. When we lose the awareness that we are supposed to be different, our relationship begins to stagnate, and we start blaming each other when things do not go the way we think they should. We get angry when our partner does not feel and see things, or communicate and respond the way we do. Shocked and feeling lonely, we may wonder who is this stranger we are involved with.

We may find ourselves disappointed again and again when our partner does not seem to love us the way we want to be loved, or affirm or support us the way we expect. Or they do not react to things the way we think they should. We may become discouraged, even alienated, when our partner responds negatively to something we favor, decides to vote for a candidate we cannot stand, handles a business matter in a way we think is wrong, or has a different approach to raising children or dealing with extended family. We are dismayed to discover that the same differences that made us special in the beginning of our relationship turn out to be the ones that cause us the most frustration and disappointment. This can undermine our trust in each other. We may wonder what happened to all the energy, excitement, and acceptance we initially brought to our relationship.

I continue by explaining that understanding and respecting each other means we have to take the time to become aware of our differences, and then learn how to appreciate our partner's uniqueness once again. Enjoying our differences adds depth and fullness to our lives. Refusing to value them leaves us feeling resentful, isolated, and intolerant. Trust and respect are quickly lost, and, if we are not committed to reclaiming the appreciation we once felt, our love will starve, wilt, and begin to die.

Opposites Attract

The love we are experiencing, like in the stories of Psyche and Eros and our other couples, begins with the truth in the old cliché that "opposites attract." Our partner catches our attention with qualities that fascinate us and frequently make us feel more complete. Unconsciously, their characteristics, and our attraction to them, often represent shadows of old wounds sustained by unresolved childhood issues— an overbearing mother, a cold, distant father, or an environment that was deficient in some vital way. Something was missing that we continue to search for in order to heal it. This new, exciting relationship contains the seeds of our healing and growth that we need to cultivate. For example, a shy, thoughtful person finds that an outgoing, lively partner brings a fresh sense of vitality and involvement into their lives. A warm, feeling person might be attracted to someone who helps bring objectivity to how they see things. Their partner may likewise value the warmth they bring in return. There are many ways we can bring new energy to each other when we fall in love.

What many people call disillusionment generally begins when the complementary aspects of the relationship start to wear off. The outgoing partner gets tired of having to initiate their social life, and even their conversations. The thoughtful partner may become irritated at the other person's unpredictable behavior, while the spontaneous one of them loses patience with his or her partner's rigidity. The very things that attracted us to each other now seem to create an abyss that can become filled with conflict, disdain, frustration, and judgment.

The key to understanding each other begins with learning some of the fundamental ways one person can be different from another. The four areas of differences are: (1) the way we prefer to approach life, (2) the way we take in information and form our point of view, (3) the way we make decisions, and (4) how much we like to be organized or open-ended.

Understanding and consciously learning to appreciate our differences helps us give and receive the love that is in our hearts. By accepting and valuing our differences, we can help each other in many areas of life, and we become more creative as a couple. In addition, we can learn the best ways of accommodating and supporting each other. We will also learn how to better understand other people in our lives.

I ask the group to keep these thoughts in mind—how opposites first attract and then collide—as we return to our story of Steve. We will see how Maggie explains these differences and how they can help love grow.

When Steve goes home, he follows Maggie's advice and asks Ann to sit down and talk with him. He tells her he feels that something is missing in their marriage. She looks stunned. Without noticing her expression, Steve goes on to explain that he had talked with a co-worker and, at length, with his cousin Maggie. To his astonishment, Ann blurts out, "Are you having an affair?" Steve sees that Maggie's prediction is correct. Ann is very upset. He does his best to use his new skills to listen to Ann until he completely understands what she is feeling. It soon becomes clear she feels furious, belittled, and betrayed because he had not talked with her first. She feels like she has worked hard to be a supportive wife and a good mother, facts she feels Steve is ignoring. Steve realizes that his own feeling of not wanting to bother Ann until he had worked this problem out has been totally wrong.

As their discussion continues, thanks to Steve's new skills, they begin to feel better. Before long Steve is sitting close to Ann with his arm around her. They feel more connected than they have for a very long time. They agree with Maggie's ideas about how attention, patience, listening, and sharing oneself show love, respect, kindness, and trust. And they agree to come back to them as soon as they have a chance to recover from their discussion.

However, Steve is struck by how Ann's fear, hurt, and anger have caught him unaware. He thinks it might be worthwhile for him to speak to Maggie again. He wants to find out more about how Maggie knew what Ann's response would be. He also begins to ask himself why he had not known how Ann would react. This question disturbs him and leaves him wondering how well he really knows her.

Steve tells Ann that he has more questions he would like to ask Maggie and suggests they meet with her together. Ann replies that while she trusts Maggie, she needs more time to think about the things she and Steve have been discussing. She suggests that Steve go ahead and talk with her if he wants to and perhaps she will join them another time.

Steve arranges to meet Maggie in the park. When he arrives, he is surprised to find her husband, Jim, with her. Jim greets him, shakes hands, and says that Maggie has told him about their conversation. He says that he wanted to join them and share the most important insight he has ever had.

Maggie smiles at Jim's enthusiasm. After they sit down, Jim continues. "Let me give you a little background information to help you see how I built up to this insight. When I fell in love with Maggie, I was drawn to her warmth and openness, and by the number of friendships she enjoyed. Once I got to know her better, I was also fascinated by her intuition. She could see through things or see possibilities before I even realized I was supposed to be looking."

Maggie takes his hand and adds that she was impressed by how stable and practical Jim was, solid and organized. They seemed to be a perfect fit.

Jim goes on to tell about finishing college, where he and Maggie had met, and about their early married life. Jim went to work in sales and business. He worked hard, but finally had to face the reality that he was miserable in his job. With Maggie's support, he went to a career counselor, where, for the first time, he was introduced to something called "psychological types."

Jim reveals that the counselor gave him a well-known personality inventory called the Myers-Briggs Type Indicator (MBTI). This inventory helps people understand what kind of situations and lifestyles energize them. It also helps them figure out the general ways they usually like to gather information, communicate, and make decisions. With the help of the MBTI, the counselor confirmed that Jim liked to work alone without someone looking over his shoulder. He enjoyed a hands-on approach to his work, liked things laid out clearly, was naturally organized, and felt satisfied by seeing immediate results.

"With the counselor's help and Maggie's support, I decided to go to our community college and become an electrician." Jim reflects that this change worked well for him and, as he became wrapped up in the pursuit of his new profession, he forgot all about psychological types. Maggie adds that they were engrossed in making a living, establishing a home, and getting started in life.

Jim continues describing his journey. "In a few years, I decided I wanted to make more money. I believed the best way to do that was to hire people and start an electrical contracting firm. Looking back I can see how this move caused me to grow. I had to learn people skills and how to make a business plan for the future." He adds that Maggie, a great people person, could see all sorts of possibilities for the future and was a big help to him. They thought they were a good team.

Jim looks like he is choosing his next words carefully. After a few moments, he says that even with all of the things they had going for them, trouble was brewing. Despite the fact that they loved each other, they began to argue over trivial things and suddenly, these disagreements erupted into vicious exchanges.

Maggie shares that she thought Jim was going out of his way to be difficult during these episodes. They were particularly awful with each other, hammering *away at the other's self-esteem. She says that she accused him of being mean, inflexible, cold, and hard-headed, and he called her impulsive, chaotic, sentimental, and irrational.*

"Suddenly," Jim says, "the very things that attracted us to each other were no longer appreciated. It seemed like I was determined to force Maggie to be just like me, and she was just as determined to make me more like her." He admits that he wanted her to be more logical and organized, and she wanted him to loosen up and become more outgoing. She also kept saying she wanted them to have a deep, meaningful relationship, while he didn't even know what that meant, even though he thought he should know. They were married, after all. One thing he was sure of was that he wanted to be appreciated for how hard he was working.

"All of a sudden there was this huge gulf between us. I felt like I didn't really know Maggie anymore. I wasn't too sure how well I knew myself, either," Jim says, shaking his head. He observes that he would get totally exasperated during their arguments. He remembers that as soon as they started, he knew they were on a destructive path but couldn't stop himself. That is when he realized they needed to separate for a while.

Maggie, listening intently, notes that the other problem was that they had gotten very attached to the image of being a happy couple. Their friends and family admired them, but they no longer admired themselves. "Even so, it took time and the threat that we were really losing each other before we could swallow our pride and go to a counselor for help," Maggie shares with sadness as she remembers their experience. After the counselor listened to them for two sessions, she stopped their discussion and explained that she believed many of their conflicts came from how different their personalities were. The counselor also pointed out that the characteristics that originally made them feel like a good team had now become points of conflict.

"I was amazed!" Jim exclaims. He then goes on to detail how the counselor explained that they needed to look beneath the surface of any conflict that seemed to open a gulf between them. There they would most likely discover that the basic difficulty they had was a difference in how they saw problems and their standpoint toward them. She also told them that while most like to think they are open-minded, deep down they believe their way is the best way, if not the only way. They base their self-esteem on this assumption and fight for it. They

become so dominated by this unconscious process that they just cannot under-
stand why their partner does not agree with them.

Jim reports that the counselor gave them a chart that generally described
basic psychological types. She reviewed the chart carefully with them and said
that sometimes they will be one way, and sometimes another, but in each pair
of characteristics, we tend to prefer one over the other most of the time. "For
example, I prefer hands-on experiences in contrast to hunches. That makes me
sensing more than intuitive."

We pause in the story to review our own chart that briefly explains what Jim
and Maggie's counselors have been talking about. We can get a rough idea of
our type by simply checking one of each pair of opposite characteristics on
the following chart.

I AM ENERGIZED BY*

—Extroversion or	**—Introversion**
activities, people, events and many friends/ acquaintances	solitude, ideas, concepts a few good friends
Extroverts prefer action	**Introverts prefer reflection**
—Sensing or	**—Intuition**
concrete, information, facts, lists, the here and now, notice details, resists change	perceives possibilities, looks beneath the surface, looks to the future, enjoys change and fantasies
Sensing types prefer hands-on experiences	**Intuitive types prefer hunches**
—Thinking or	**—Feeling**
making logical, objective, impersonal decisions	making decisions based on how much you care and how they matter to other people
Thinking types act from the head	**Feeling types act from the heart**
—Judging or	**—Perceiving**
Living an orderly, well-organized or controlled life	Living in a way that is flexible, adaptive and goes with the flow
Judging types like being organized	**Perceiving types like being open-ended**

* The four preferences scored to generate types on the Myers-Briggs Type Indicator
(adapted from the Type Table in the *Type Reporter*, 1986, 3/2)

In my case, for example, because I am energized by activities, people, events, and social activities, I would check *extroversion*. That does not mean I never like to be alone or to sit and think. It simply means I am more energized by activity and interactions with people.

Barry notes that he has seen something like this before. They had a consultant at his office come to help them learn to work together as a team. She used the Myers-Briggs test. Cory adds that they looked at a similar test at her workplace.

Massimilla explains that the MBTI gives more complete information than our basic chart. The idea is not to categorize, but to help us better understand ourselves and to see ways we may be different from each other.

This helps several members of the group, who announce that they do not like the idea of being categorized, and do not believe that they can be sized up that easily.

I remind them that we are not trying to pigeonhole anyone. Studying how we can be different from each other helps us let go of hidden assumptions that other people see and respond to things the way we do.

Tom volunteers that this is one of those things he understands in his head but has trouble remembering when he is dealing with people. "Oh, that's so true!" Cindy agrees.

Massimilla wants everyone to be clear that we all need to really understand what we are talking about. She points out that most of us are going to be attracted to someone who is different from us in several fundamental ways. When we discover that our soul mate may actually see things differently, have different priorities and values, and does not seem to understand or respect ours, we may feel deeply betrayed. Yet once we have learned how to use the valuable resources and tools we have been discussing, we remember that what we have in common is a relationship based on love, respect, kindness, and trust. That is far more important than being psychological twins.

Vanessa, while admitting this is a very important point, remains skeptical about being sized up so easily.

I agree with her that it is not that easy to figure ourselves out. Our choices in the categories that energize us are influenced by a variety of things: our families, school, work, physical characteristics, and so on. The idea we want to bookmark as far as our relationships are concerned is to learn how to appreciate our differences. We must discover how to keep them from remaining reasons for conflict rather than challenges to grow. We must move from conflict to growth. That is a very important part of our journey to love.

With a sudden burst of understanding, Jim observes that it is easy to see how different they are. He is introverted, sensing, and thinking. Maggie is extraverted, intuitive, and feeling. They are split about equally between judging and perceiving. He asks the counselor if their relationship is impossible.

She laughs and tells him that she does not think that is the right question. She says that first understanding our differences are legitimate, and that we can still have love in common should take a lot of the pressure off of our relationship. Most of the time, this awareness helps us begin to appreciate each other again and to look for more common ground.

Jim shares with Steve that the minute he realized their differences were not intentional and based on animosity, he felt like a huge weight had been lifted off his shoulders. He also adds that their counselor advised them to remember that it is important not to relate to other people as if they are just like us.

Do not relate to other people as if they are just like you

Their counselor also told them that we generally develop the characteristics that are the most natural to us. But we have the capacity to use and enjoy all of them to some extent. The ones we use the least can often be a little awkward or clumsy simply because we have not taken the time and effort to become skilled in them.

Jim explains to Steve how this has played out in his own life. "You should see me trying to speak in public. I am terrified when I have to present a report to my professional association."

Jim goes on to say that while this is a common challenge for an introvert, they can learn to enjoy public speaking. Some have become politicians, even presidents. Maggie adds that the characteristics that attracted her to Jim, his reserve, practicality, and solidity, are also potentials in her. She learned that eventually she will have to develop those parts of herself.

Wishing to better understand, Steve asks, "Is that the idea? To find middle ground and live together there?"

Maggie responds that, in most relationships, each person begins to get tired of carrying the whole burden in a particular area. "I wanted Jim to begin initiating some of our social life. And Jim wanted me to plan some quiet time at home." She says she also had to realize Jim needs to be alone sometimes without worrying about whether or not she feels neglected.

Jim agrees that this was an important insight. "We had a few feisty discussions in those areas."

Maggie admits that while she is not perfect, she is steadily improving. "For years, Jim wanted me to be more organized, to plan meals in advance, keep the checkbook balanced, and clothes put away." She acknowledges her progress, and shares that while she may never enjoy those things, she does enjoy the fact that her marriage is better and stronger for it.

We pause to emphasis that mastering something that is difficult personally, and challenging in a relationship, often gives us a sense of pride and deep satisfaction. We also note that it is easier, and more enjoyable, to make that stretch when we know our partner is not simply being obstinate about our behavior. Then it feels like a loving thing to do, rather than a capitulation. When we are working together harmoniously, we can often divide things up so each can do what they do, or like to do, best.

I ask the group if anyone feels like they carry the whole burden of one of these areas in their relationship. Trish immediately answers, "You bet!" She goes on to explain that she thinks Bob is so introverted he simply gets overwhelmed trying to plan or figure out the comings and goings of their children, not to mention visitation days and holidays. Both of his children are in high school, play sports year-round, and visit their mother every other weekend; her two middle-schoolers play soccer and swim. They have practices afternoons and evenings, games or meets every time they turn around, car-pools, and who knows *when* they can actually plan a family meal together. Trish takes a breath and then finishes by admitting that there are other things to manage, like shopping, or that Bob and she need an evening to themselves.

Everyone agrees when Cory exclaims, "Whew! And I thought our lives were hectic."

Bob responds that he knows he has to help her more with their scheduling nightmare, but he admits that it is frustrating for him to try to keep up with so many details.

Massimilla asks him if he is more sensing or intuitive, and he replies that he is intuitive.

Based on his response, she tells him that he may need to make a plan, or a calendar, something concrete, to hold all of the details of their children's schedules. She also advises him to remember that he is performing a "sensing" chore that he normally does not like to do and that does not come easily to him. But once he has started he may enjoy getting more control over the situation, and enjoy the involvement he will get to share with his family. "Perhaps you and Trish could do it together. Then let everyone know, especially the children, that you are not going to be very flexible. I would plan at least a month at a time. Include your children in the planning and let them know how much advance warning you need to make any changes. This is a difficult, complex issue that you have to control concretely, or it can, as you have already experienced, become so complicated, everyone will be stressed out and resentful."

In response to Trish's question about the appropriateness of being that structured with other people's lives, Massimilla assures her that they have to be. They have to protect their relationship, minimize the conflict between the two of them over children's schedules and having to coordinate with former spouses, not to mention to give themselves the space to love each other. If they do not, everyone will lose.

I join with Massimilla and emphasize that in emotionally loaded situations, it is better to be specific and logical to help keep guilt, resentments, and old regrets out of the picture. For example, Trish and Bob will want to make sure that they, and each child, get considered in the planning. Doing so does not mean they have to be cold or distant. It means they have to be aware and intentional in helping each other handle the situation. The children can be included, but they do not run the show. Protecting the space for love does not mean they do not love the children. It means they are modeling a healthy, balanced, adult relationship.

Trish says that this perspective is helpful. "I always feel guilty when I want Bob to spend time with me instead of going to one of his children's games. But in other situations, even though I know Bob cares deeply for his children, I seem to be more tuned in to how his children are feeling. I believe Bob ignores how angrily his son Josh responds to him and how withdrawn his daughter Liz has become." She confesses that she wants Bob to pay attention, listen to her, and do something about it.

Bob looks startled by what he hears. He acknowledges that she is absolutely right. "I did not really believe you. I thought they were just being teenagers. But you are right. I need to pay attention to what you are able to see that I can't."

I point out that this situation highlights a common difference between an extrovert's response—Trish's—and that of an introvert—Bob. I describe how this is another example of how the story of Eros and Psyche is useful. I ask them to imagine for a minute that Bob is Eros and Trish is Psyche. Once Trish gets fed up enough with this issue, she will get angry and burn Bob in an effort to shed light on this subject. A positive outcome requires that both of them change. Bob must make the effort to be more aware of feelings in the outer world, and Trish will have to give him the space to do this self-discovery while both of them mature in their ability to understand each other.

The room is quiet for a moment. Then Cory confides that she and Barry have a different kind of problem. She explains that as a carryover from her banking days, she feels they need to take better care of their finances. She is beginning to feel like Barry is abandoning her in this responsibility.

Barry is incredulous and marvels at what she has said. "We talk about our budget and agree on our major expenditures. You even keep the books and pay the bills."

While Cory concedes that this is true, she asks him to recall a recent night when they discussed his debit card. "I never know what's coming on the statement at the end of the month. Sometimes I feel like you're too intuitive and feeling. If you want to buy something nice for the children or me, you buy it. That's great—it gives you pleasure, all of us pleasure. But then you just assume, intuitively I suppose, that I'll be able to balance the books. The pressure to clean up after you is on me."

Barry looks as though he has really heard what Cory has to say. Michael ventures that finances must be a real potential snake pit for different types.

I agree and offer a helpful option by saying that the best thing we can do is to figure out how we are different, and how we can work together in this area. There is a danger of Cory feeling forced into the position of a stern parent when Barry buys something, while Barry could feel hurt or treated like an irresponsible child when he tries to do something special and it is not appreciated. Barry and Cory, like most of us, need to carefully talk these issues through until we are clear about how to help and honor each other.

Before we return to the story of Jim, Steve, and Maggie, Massimilla emphasizes that we can see, in each of these cases, how one person can feel especially burdened. Growing respect for each other and for understanding our differences are crucial. So is using our intimacy skills to facilitate the process. Massimilla explains to Bob how he can develop his capacity for details to help take some of the burden off Trish. She tells Barry that he needs to use more of his sensing and thinking capacity so he will not buy things impulsively, albeit lovingly. He may need to learn to keep a concrete record in order to monitor his own spending.

Jim says, "I wanted to join Maggie today just to tell you what a relief it was when I discovered that the source of our conflicts was not a failure in our relationship."

Maggie shares that she really liked the promise of change and potential the new typology offered them. She saw it as a chance to rebuild and renew their relationship. "To learn we could focus on appreciating each other again, and laugh at some of our differences. I wished we had learned these things before we hurt each other so much. That is why Jim and I are so happy to share what we have learned with you and Ann."

Steve responds that he is very grateful. He tells them how helpful and generous they have been. After a moment, he confesses that he has another question. He wants to know if their style of dealing with their psychological type affects how they hear and understand each other. "How do you keep from having misunderstandings?"

Maggie replies that it does affect them, but the trick is to keep tossing the ball back and forth in a respectful way. She says that her rule is to not argue until she has sincerely tried to find out what Jim means. She needs to listen to Jim carefully, and then respond in a respectful manner.

Jim adds that being patient when your partner is trying to understand you is very important. They are not trying to insult us. He reflects that understanding their differences is like building another bridge between them.

"If we don't recognize and value our differences," Maggie explains, "neither feels respected for who we really are. We either end up stalemated, bending over backwards to accommodate the other, or throwing up defensive walls." She shares that when that happens, they lose their ability to be loving and end up resentful and lonely. Jim grins and says that while Maggie is right, she makes it sound a little severe. He takes a more positive approach and says that learning to appreciate each other expands their ability to love.

Learning to appreciate each other expands our ability to love

Jim shares that their counselor told them most couples differ on only one or two characteristics, and this should make it easier to talk things through and find middle ground. After a long pause Steve says that their conversation has been very enlightening, but a lot to take in and process. He wants to know how—once Ann and he have figured out their differences, learned how to communicate, and show appreciation and respect for each other —they can make the really tough decisions.

Maggie jumps in and tells Steve that by the time they have thoroughly discussed a topic these days, they have usually arrived at a decision. If they have not, they try to figure out what kind of decision needs to be made. Is it one from the head, the heart, or both? And what does it affect: the present or the future? They try to approach it as a team.

"For example, how we decide to invest our retirement account is primarily a head issue. How much can we save now? What do we want to have later?" Maggie admits that there is a secondary heart issue for her. She wants to invest in companies that respect people and the environment. There may not be a perfect solution, but they have to respect each other and do the best they can.

Maggie explains that there are some situations where she needs Jim's logic and clarity. She shares that a few weeks before, her mother wanted to come stay with them for a month. She got so mixed up in her feelings between what she thought she should do and how she really felt, and how saying "no" would make her mother feel, that she almost dissolved in tears. Then Jim stepped in with his logic and practicality, and reminded her of their other commitments and how they felt after her last visit. "Now, his intervention is a precious gift. In the past when I was so stuck and miserable, I would have felt he did not understand my dilemma. I would have rejected his help and could have even turned it into a fight."

Before they say goodbye, Maggie wants to know if she was right about how Ann would feel. Steve answers that she was absolutely right, and asks if the four of them can get together soon. Maggie enthusiastically says that they have a plan!

Introversion vs. Extroversion: A Different Way of Being in Life

—Extroversion	**—Introversion**
activities, people, events and many friends/ acquaintances	solitude, ideas, concepts a few good friends
Extroverts prefer action	**Introverts prefer reflection**

Many in the group agree that the story has touched some chords, and most identify with the couples in the story. Trish begins by acknowledging that the couple could have been her and Bob. When she met him, she saw still waters running deep; now all she can see is a dry riverbed.

Cory chimes in that she knows exactly how Trish feels. "Barry is pretty introverted, but I like to talk all the time. I talk to think things through. When we met, he thought I was vivacious. But now, my talking irritates him, and he either does not respond or he makes fun of me. I just hate it when I can see he is upset or angry and he won't tell me why."

Trish agrees, and affirms that Cory understands why it is so frustrating. She is sick of saying, "Hello, I'm here!"

I want to emphasize that their points are important. Whether we are introverts or simply do not want to upset our partners, we are making a mistake when we do not share our frustrations and feelings. Not only do we deny our partner the chance to be understanding and helpful, but we may also be giving them the impression they are the source of our problems. Massimilla adds that extroverts are particularly vulnerable in this area because they are more aware of what is going on around them.

Karen asks Cory why she thinks she was attracted to an introvert. After considering the question, Cory truthfully replies that she is not sure she would even like being with another extrovert; they might be too competitive for airtime.

Clearly, this discussion is having an impact on Bob. He speaks up and confesses that he has spent most of his life feeling like something was wrong with him. "I'm not shy. I talk to people at work all day. But I get tired of talking and being 'on.' I need some time to rest, to relax. Being in a blended family isn't helpful in that aspect either. I thought we were well suited, too. I believed Trish admired my quiet approach to things." He pauses and then shares that he is not mean and he is not critical. He strongly feels that Trish is over-reacting.

I tell the group that Bob is not alone in his feelings. Our culture is so geared to being outgoing and action-oriented that our quieter members often feel like something is wrong with them. Massimilla wants the group to remember that regardless of whether we are introverts or extroverts, we all have to talk things through in order to feel close and connected.

"I'm the introvert in our relationship," Cindy volunteers. "Unfortunately, years ago I was also a pleaser. And, like Bob, I always felt like something was wrong with me." She admits that she put on a big act of enjoying sports events and parties to accommodate Tom, and to be more like she thought she was supposed to be. She pauses as she considers her next words carefully. "Then one day, a few years after we were married, I felt like I had disappeared in our relationship and I was feeling very resentful. With the help of a therapist, I realized I was okay. Introversion is just another way of living. I didn't need to change myself or to feel guilty."

Tom adds that it was a big relief for him, too. He knew Cindy was unhappy. They hit some rough spots when she began to change and quit doing things she did not like. "Sometimes, I would feel hurt and surprised. But as she did more things she wanted to, her confidence grew and we began to genuinely enjoy more activities together. I think our experience helped us to appreciate how much pleasure we can have with each other when we both are understood and respected."

Massimilla reflects that being sensitive to each other is important, but being a pleaser can devour us. It means we are afraid we are not good enough, or that our self-esteem is too dependent on other people's responses. It can also mean we over-emphasize appearances. We do not want conflict to mar our ideal of the good relationship.

There is a pause as people think about these remarks.

Then Cindy says, "I still get a little jealous when I see Tom's huge network of friends and acquaintances that range from work to little-league coaching. If I'm not careful, I end up feeling secondary." She adds that she also wants more time to herself, or time with a few of her friends. She recognizes that what is important is for her to remember that Tom loves her, and if she is feeling lonely, she needs to let him know. Tom readily admits that he gets distracted, but he thinks they get along much better now.

Leah promptly agrees and identifies with Cindy. "I am clearly an introvert and on the quiet side, while Karen is on the nervous, active side." When Karen asks her what she means by nervous, Leah responds that Karen's activities and many friends seems nervous to her. She also notes that they need to remember that they balance each other out, and to not let their differences be threatening.

I stress that extroversion and introversion frequently are challenging to deal with because they easily can become conflicting lifestyles. I point out that Cindy prefers a quieter, more reflective lifestyle, while Tom likes to be out there interacting with lots of people. Our culture complicates this situation because it places more value on an approach like Tom's. This leaves us quieter people feeling a bit left out and inferior. But in reality, a balanced life needs both extroversion and introversion. I admit that though I am somewhat of an introvert, I am more extroverted than Massimilla. The only way I know to solve these conflicts with her is by talking them out. We can reconcile most differences when we listen without hostility, and strive to understand each other. Trish asks if we can give them a few tips, so Massimilla writes the following tips on the board while I describe tips for both introverts and extroverts, while reminding the group that both types need to remember to toss the ball gently so both can feel successful.

Tips for the Introvert

1. Share good qualities you notice, and appreciate, about your partner.

2. Make the effort to articulate concerns, ideas, and feelings.

3. When your partner is upset, listen actively, rather than shutting down or tuning out.

Tips for the Extrovert

1. Accept that the other is less talkative than you and that they are not being critical or stubborn.

2. Be ready to listen when they are ready to talk. When an introvert is ready to talk, let them do it in their own deliberate way.

3. Don't interrupt, try to speed up the process, or quickly say what you think.

4. Approach important topics calmly, and do not press for quick answers.

Cory remarks that if these differences are so important to adults then we really need to be careful to figure out our children and not make them feel bad about who they are.

Massimilla responds by explaining that these skills will expand beyond our intimate relationship and will enhance our relationships with other family members, friends, coworkers, and beyond. She also shares that, for our friendships, we are more likely to be attracted to people who are similar to us, but that understanding one another is an important part of any relationship.

Sensing vs. Intuitive: A Different Way of Processing

—Sensing	—Intuition
concrete, information, facts, lists, the here and now, notice details, resists change	perceives possibilities, looks beneath the surface, looks to the future, enjoys change and fantasies
Sensing types prefer hands-on experiences	**Intuitive types prefer hunches**

I begin this discussion by pointing out that if introversion and extroversion are like lifestyles, then sensing and intuition make up our perspective on things. Barry guesses that this may be the next biggest area of disagreement after introversion and extroversion, and where he and Cory bump up against one another.

Trish, lightly teasing Bob, says, "You mean intuitives like Bob have a hard time dealing with practical matters?" Tom smiles and adds that if sensing is practical and hands-on, then Cindy is the earth mother. Leah inserts that while Karen is concrete and practical, she is no earth mother.

Bob responds that he identifies with Jim in the story; he likes facts and being logical, and trusts his own experiences or hunches.

Massimilla and I ask the group to notice how difficult it is to classify, or pigeonhole, all behaviors as a certain type. I add that this system is most helpful when we use it to explore our behavior and that of our partners with the intention of better understanding what motivates our thoughts, feelings, and actions. This nurtures the process of understanding and appreciation.

Trish articulates her style of relating. "I not only talk all the time, but I'm also intuitive. And let me tell you, if you want to make a thinking person mad, start talking to him about your dreams, or the hundred different things you could do on vacation, or being unhappy with things the way they are."

Bob heartily agrees. "I think we're happy and then Trish starts talking about how she wants to change everything."

I respond that they are right. Sensing types and many thinking types want to live a happy, stable life, and intuitives are very willing to change things because they feel the future can be better.

Massimilla adds that most of us who are intuitive do not want to be bothered by thinking about the present. Leah responds that while she feels they make a good team, Karen is more pessimistic than she is.

I observe that change needs to be digested by sensing types. They may tend to see it negatively at first. But then they can become very optimistic. Buying a new house initially may look like a way to invite chaos and the overwhelming job of packing and moving into their lives. Sensing types have to work through this perspective before they can move beyond it and appreciate how the move might improve their lives. But in my experience, sensing people are more aware of happiness and sadness while intuitives are more alert to being sensitive or insensitive.

Trish expresses that their differences in intuition and sensing were as much to blame as being introverted and extroverted. "Just like in the story of Maggie and Jim, I think Bob is disorganized and untidy, and he thinks I'm rigid and hypercritical. But from what you are saying, these are natural differences that we misunderstand or misinterpret in each other."

I agree, and note that we have to remember: our differences are meant to help us get out of our rut and to become more open and creative. When we can understand and rebalance the energy patterns in our relationships, we feel more at home with each other. This brings us to the next pattern: thinking versus feeling.

Thinking vs. Feeling:
A Different Way of Making Decisions

—Thinking	—Feeling
making logical, objective, impersonal decisions	making decisions based on how much you care and how they matter to other people
Thinking types act from the head	**Feeling types act from the heart**

Barry asks to delve into thinking and feeling because he thinks they have stumbled a lot on this one in the past. "Cindy is not the only pleaser in this group."

Vanessa picks up the ball and asks Barry if he is the thinker or the feeler. "I'm the feeler," Barry answers.

Cory tells us she likes that about Barry. "I was really attracted to his warmth and humor. Even so, for a while we were fighting as much as Jim and Maggie were. Barry is very expressive and sympathetic, but if I make a negative comment about anyone anywhere in the world he gets angry and calls me cold and judgmental."

Barry admits that fairness is a big concern. He can see that there are times Cory is only trying to make conversation. And he recognizes that he gets caught up trying to defend the underdog, even when there is no attack going on, or it does not matter. "But sometimes Cory is so rational and on point I don't think she is considering the people involved."

"You have told me I was a big help during those times when you felt stuck because you were too worried about upsetting people," Cory counters. "Like the time I helped you turn down the huge hassle of being chairman of fund-raising for your alumni group. I know you're smart and it irritates me to see you get stuck that way."

Barry admits that this is very true. He also reflects that she has saved him more than once. "It's not unlike what Jim did for Maggie when her mother wanted to visit." After pausing for a moment Barry adds that he knows what a loving person Cory is and wishes that she would show that side of herself more often.

Leah wants to know how the two of them maintain their relationship in light of the difficulties they just shared.

Cory confesses that understanding the real source of some of their differences would have saved them a lot of stress and strain. Like looking for the things they appreciate about each other and building on their strengths instead of fighting about their differences.

"I think this new awareness definitely is going to help us handle the children better, too," Barry says. "Cory probably needs to help me be a little firmer, and I may need to help her soften up a bit."

Massimilla and I are very pleased with the awareness, honesty, understanding, and insight the group is bringing to our discussion. I ask the group to continue to look for ways they can help each other bring balance to their situation instead of criticizing how they see the other person doing it.

Trish, grinning, says, "I remember an accounting class I took during business school. It was a nightmare for me. Learning about thinking and feeling helps me understand why. One day, just before finals, I was so frustrated I broke down in tears in my professor's office. I must have scared him to death. That poor man did not know what to do with feelings."

Barry, laughing, tells us that if we think that's funny, we should have seen him, an intuitive, feeling type trying to explain to a mechanic what was wrong with his car. The mechanic went into a trance.

Now, everyone is laughing. At this point, Michael speaks up. I notice that neither he nor Vanessa have contributed to this part of the discussion.

He admits that he is getting worried because Vanessa and he are alike on almost all of their decision-making. Vanessa agrees and asks if that means they are in trouble because they will not experience as many opportunities for growth.

When Massimilla replies that she thinks Vanessa and Michael will have to work harder to develop themselves, Vanessa, appearing genuinely curious, asks her to elaborate.

"It means you could get caught in a pattern of mistakes because neither of you can see all of the available alternatives," Massimilla replies. "For example, if you are both sensing, you may find it hard to plan for the future. If you are both intuitive, you may lose track of some daily tasks like keeping your checkbook balanced or the due-dates of bills. You may also get in a rut without realizing it. You may find it gets too comfortable to keep doing the same things day after day. This complacency and boredom can eventually make something or someone outside of your relationship look unrealistically interesting."

I acknowledge that Massimilla's insights, while a response to the specific concerns of Vanessa and Michael, can be applied to any relationship and particular type that fits this description. Before we move on, I want to emphasis that, generally we find the old saying that "opposites attract" is true for most people. In the rare instances where both people in a relationship are alike, there is the danger of falling into a kind of brother-sister or sibling relationship. While this may make the relationship initially seem more peaceful, it is harder to stimulate growth in each other, as well as within themselves. If they are not very intentional and committed to growing, outside attractions to other people, careers, hobbies, and so on, can absorb attention and drain love from the relationship. Comfort truly can be their enemy.

There is a danger, too, of becoming competitive or resentful. In some cases, people who are too similar end up letting one person dominate in the relationship, and the other will eventually resent being the weaker party.

I share that not too long ago, I began working with a deeply distressed couple. The wife controlled the money and most of their activities, and eventually, the husband grew sarcastic and critical and their relationship turned hostile. Instead of seeking help, they both reinforced their positions and she held on to her controlling strategy. Then she discovered her husband was having an affair. It is going to take a lot of work for them to heal their wounds and transform their relationship, or to separate and become people with the potential to love again.

Massimilla adds, reassuringly, that one of the advantages of being similar types is that they have a natural kind of friendliness. They can be a good support for helping each other grow. She instructs the group not to forget that we are all individuals. Just because we both choose "thinking" does not mean we are going to think alike. It only means we follow a similar process for making decisions. She then asks Vanessa and Michael if they are different on any of the other categories.

Judging vs. Perceiving: A Different Way of Living

—Judging	—Perceiving
Living an orderly, well-organized or controlled life	Living in a way that is flexible, adaptive and goes with the flow
Judging types like being organized	**Perceiving types like being open-ended**

Michael quickly answers that Vanessa is judging while he is perceiving. Massimilla responds that this can be a pretty big difference no matter how much they are alike in other ways. Vanessa will have a real feeling of urgency about having things finished, under control, and decisions made.

Vanessa rolls her eyes at Michael and says, "That's right. I like to plan my days and feel like I'm focused and getting things accomplished. I don't enjoy having things disrupt my plan. But that doesn't mean I can't be spontaneous, have fun, or handle a crisis. It just means I enjoy being focused."

I tell Michael that Vanessa may also push for closure while he holds out for more information. He may even hope that if he holds out long enough, the problem will go away.

"Sometimes it does," Tom adds, with a laugh.

Michael brags about Vanessa's work ethic in the kitchen. He tells us that everything is carefully prepared, ready on time, and cleaned up—ready for inspection. Then he expands his admiration to her work ethic at her job, too.

Vanessa tells us what a disaster the kitchen scene is with Michael in charge. She teases him by saying that the food is good if you can find it in the mess!

"Don't worry. It sounds like you have your growthful challenges cut out for you!" Cindy says good-naturedly.

Vanessa is quick to add that she admires that Michael does not get up-tight with her need to plan. He is very flexible and able to go with the flow.

The group is quiet. I want to acknowledge that while this meeting has been a very good one, it has touched some very sensitive nerves. We all have things to think about and sort through. I remind them how easy and natural it is to assume that our partner's reactions, needs, and desires are the same as our own. Slipping into this assumption will generally lead to misunderstanding, resentment, and rejection. But learning to understand our differences can help us renew our love and treasure each other's uniqueness. Appreciating our differences can help us remember the strength of love's mystery as it works to open our hearts and leads us into a more satisfying life and a relationship we can trust.

5

COURAGE AND STRENGTH: THE CRAFT OF MOVING FROM FEAR TO TRUST

Fear is the question. What are you afraid of and why? Just as the seed of health is in illness, because illness contains information, our fears are a treasure house of self-knowledge if we explore them.
—Marilyn Ferguson

We greet each other warmly on the morning of our last meeting, a day that seems to have come too quickly. The topic today is courage and strength: moving from fear to trust. Before we return to the story of Jim, Maggie, Steve, and Ann, I introduce the topic.

When a new relationship deepens, we usually think, or at least hope, we now are secure. Slowly, as we build our lives around being together, we often take our bond for granted and do not notice small, potentially threatening changes when they begin to occur. Once we do finally notice that important matters between us are out of alignment, we become afraid, angry, or despairing as did Eros and Psyche. Our feelings are understandable but not very helpful.

The more important our relationship is to us, the more tightly we hold onto it. We may try to deny what is happening, become a pleaser in our efforts to maintain peace and harmony, or act aggressive and angry in an effort to force our partner back into our old "safe" patterns. These attempts are also understandable although they usually are hurtful, even destructive. It is important to remember that relationships are a journey, and hope blossoms as we grow to a new level of intimacy.

We often are afraid and easily fall into blaming each other for the situation we find ourselves in. In addition, we may feel we have invested too much, are too old to change, or do not want to risk being made a fool of. Yet unless we face our fears, the potential in our relationship can be buried by conflict, smothered by an uneasy truce, or hidden by our determination to maintain a pleasant facade.

I point out that we experience a great awakening when we realize we are being held captive by our fear. We are all afraid of failing and losing what we have. The threat of failing in a relationship can cause us to imagine all kinds of scary scenarios: being old and alone, broke, overwhelmed, or back in the singles market again. It may even cause us to hate, or feel repulsed by, the very idea of relationship. One reason the story of Eros and Psyche is so reassuring is that it offers us hope and freedom from fear.

The story illustrates how a new life together first begins, and then evolves into being unhappy, burned, and withdrawing from each other. This leads to a crisis we think will mean the end of a relationship, rather than a path toward a whole new beginning.

To emphasize the importance of stories to help us in our journey, I share a story about a couple in an earlier seminar who were able to identify with Eros and Psyche. The husband was afraid of being burned by his wife's anger. As they learned to talk more openly, his wife discovered the depth of his fear of anger, a fear that began as a child when he was the victim of his mother's fiery rages. He in turn began to understand his wife's fear of icy cold rejection, which she had felt as a child whenever she did not please her parents. When this couple experienced frustration in their relationship, their old fears paralyzed them. The story of Eros and Psyche helped them to realize that no matter how bad they felt, they must start the journey of sorting out their feelings so they can understand and get a better perspective on them. Journaling helped them get started and by our third meeting they were able to talk over their emotions and better understand what they meant.

Intimate communication—the value, respect, kindness, and trust we show each other—strengthens our hope and protects us against fear. As we move toward growth and share ourselves, we are better able to shift our focus from what we may lose to *what we may gain*. With every hardship she overcame, Psyche gained strength and became more capable of love. So did Eros. Embracing the journey likewise helps release us from fear.

To find our own way beyond our comforts and confront our fears, we need to help each other as we learn to understand our differences, treat each other with respect, and talk together about the things that are most important to us.

Today we are going to see how we can turn our fear into trust by learning more about what frightens us and what instills us with the courage we need to change and grow. Much of the fear and conflict we experience are based on patterns we all share to some degree. Now we will return one last time to the story of Steve and see what else he and Ann can learn from Maggie and Jim.

Jim and Maggie join Steve and Ann at their home a few weeks later on a Saturday afternoon. Ann tells Jim and Maggie how encouraging it is to hear how much they have learned from their experiences, and to see how well they are doing. She says that they have given the word "commitment" a whole new definition for her, and that she is happy to be joining the conversation about relationships.

Maggie responds that she was glad Steve had shared their conversations with Ann. Then she explains that she and Jim have carefully considered what to bring up next.

Jim tells them that they have concluded that fear was the main source of their failure to stay in tune with each other. They discovered fear was a tough area to talk about. "We can be afraid of so many things that it's often hard to narrow it down. Fear of failure scares me the most. I don't want to think of myself as a failure, nor do I want to look like a failure to Maggie, our friends, or our families."

Admitting that she often feels the same way, Maggie tells Steve and Ann that fear of failure is a big reason they both held on to the appearance of having a good relationship, even until they were at each other's throats. "We were afraid to go to counseling because we were afraid that our families and friends might think we were a failure at our relationship. Talk about a double fear whammy! We were afraid of failing at our relationship, and we were afraid of what other people think."

Jim responds that once they were in counseling, they realized it takes strength to ask for help instead of trying to hide their unhappiness. To their surprise, the people in their couples' group were not sick or dysfunctional. "They were good people like us, struggling to love each other in a complicated, stressful world."

Maggie discloses that in her most vulnerable moments, her imagination flooded her with fears. The feelings ranged from a horrible divorce fight to someday ending up old and alone. "These kinds of fears are destructive because they help convince you to settle for an unfulfilling life, rather than grow. But for me, the worst fear was rejection. My fear that Jim would stop loving me."

Maggie explains that fear put them on a path that eroded, and nearly ended, their relationship. Out of fear they began doing all the wrong things. Jim began trying to placate her instead of listening. She gave in to him at the wrong times and began to feel bullied by his moodiness and anger. In spite of the fact that they were afraid of any kind of conflict, they still seemed compelled to badger and nag each other around to their point of view.

"Of course," Jim says, "that meant we never got to the bottom of anything, and we became more and more touchy. Like Maggie said, even though we felt like we were walking on eggs around each other, we began to argue all the time."

*Fear Causes Us To
Do The Wrong Things*

Massimilla affirms that we all know how fear can imprison us. First it makes us ignore reality. Then we are taught to put on a positive face. She then recalls the line from *The King and I:* "Whenever I feel afraid, I whistle a happy tune." We whistle so no one will see our fear. But what makes this song truly haunting is that we do it so *we* will not see that we are afraid. Eventually fear makes us defensive, hostile, and aggressive. Love turns into a power struggle. Fear destroys intimacy because we will substitute manipulation for honesty. We are afraid that if we are open, our openness and honesty somehow will be used against us. Then where do we find ourselves? What is lonelier than a relationship gone cold?

I add that it also can mean that simply stating how we feel can seem as if we are starting a fight.

Steve and Ann have been listening intensely to Maggie and Jim. Steve tells Ann that he has not thought about the part fear plays between them. He has not told her about his feelings of dissatisfaction because he is afraid of upsetting her.

Ann knew something was wrong, but she did not say anything about it because she was afraid Steve was mad at her.

Maggie reminds us that it is important to see how easily fear alienates us if we are not careful. We need to remember that simply looking at issues openly is the great magic formula for growth. "You two have just shared and looked at your fears in a respectful atmosphere and it has altered the quality of them. That's something else we learned from counseling."

*Facing Fear
Changes It*

There is a moment of silence and then I observe that talking about fear reminds me of another important misconception that we often hear from couples. Many people believe they have to accept their partner totally for who they are, and instead work to change themselves. We have found this idea to be too simplistic and can be unhealthy for a relationship. For example, if our partner were an alcoholic, would we not ask them to change? Of course we would.

Massimilla, to further explain this, notes that if our partner is doing something self-destructive, we should ask them to change. A behavior that is self-destructive also will be destructive to the relationship. "For instance, if Bud is too self-critical or too critical of me, I can ask him to stop."

When Bob asks what happens if Bud does not want to, or refuses to stop the behavior, Massimilla replies that we have to explore the situation using the skills we have learned about intimate communication, and that it is helpful to remember the analogy of tossing the ball back and forth in an atmosphere of love, respect, kindness, and trust. While she can ask Bud to change things that are offensive, or hurtful to her, she should not ask him to change something authentic about himself.

"For example, I do not like it when Bud walks around the house without shaving on the weekend. And Bud does not like it when I let my desk, which is in the middle of the house, overflow with unopened mail, receipts, and old catalogs. These are examples of learned behaviors that we can change to please our partner without sacrificing a vital part of who we are."

Bud adds that many people they work with have pet peeves about their partners. Some men do not pick up after themselves, walk around with their shirts off, do not let their spouse get a word in edgewise, chew with their mouths open, pass gas, leave toilet seats up, and so on. Some women use the excuse of wanting to be comfortable in order to lounge around in warm-up suits and let their hair go. Many little things can be offensive to our partner's idea of polite and courteous behavior. Occasionally we have to decide whether a habit is truly offensive and needs to be addressed, or is simply an unpleasant aspect that may arise when two people live closely together. We have worked out a rule of thumb about this. If the habit interferes with our desire to be around the other person, or makes us look at them with disdain, we think it needs to be openly faced. We are better off in the long run to ask each other to change these things. It would be childish if we refuse to change and allow petty things to be more important than our partner's feelings. In these cases being willing to change shows love, as does asking someone to change.

At this point, I pause again, and then elaborate that being willing to change shows love, broadens our perspective, and increases good will.

Being Willing to Change Shows Love

Massimilla adds that asking someone to change is a sensitive matter. We need to be careful that we stick to offensive or destructive behaviors and that we toss the first ball to them gently and respectfully. If we feel like we need to ask for a general makeover or a more fundamental change, it usually means we have lost our ability to have an intimate discussion.

Karen and several others want to know what we should do if the other person will not change.

"Good question," Massimilla answers. "That puts the ball back in our court and we may have to decide how much of a struggle we want to make over a particular issue. If it is a serious matter, we may need to take it to a counselor. Learning to have the strength and courage to face our relationship and get the help we need is part of a loving relationship."

Moody and Opinionated: Poison for Relationships

After we take a short break, Maggie picks up the conversation and begins by saying that they really appreciate the way their counselor explained two of the most destructive moods that can seem to take possession of them like an evil spirit. He calls them Moody and Opinionated. "When one of us falls into one mood, the other partner frequently falls into the opposite one. Then the battle is on and no one can stop it. It reminds me of Merlin meeting the witch in the movie The Sword and the Stone. Whenever the two would meet, a power struggle ignited and they would destroy everything around them, with neither ever winning. They would simply wreck the cottage, destroy the forest, or wherever they happened to be near. This movie aptly symbolizes the power these moods have to make us afraid of each other.

Steve says that he thinks he knows what they are talking about, but asks for an example.

Grinning and glancing at Maggie, Jim describes a particular one that happened when they were working together in their yard. Jim had wanted the day off to play golf, but he had promised Maggie he would help get the yard in shape. Jim was trimming the shrubbery when Maggie came over and said, "No, not like that. That's too square; round them off like this," and took the clippers out of Jim's hand and showed him what she meant.

Jim immediately felt deflated. He could feel his energy draining as if a spell had been cast on him. A few minutes later, he was washing the shutters when Maggie said, in her top sergeant voice, "Don't do it that way! You're splashing the windows." At that point, Jim shook his head and muttered that nothing he ever did satisfied her.

"I hate that kind of hurt, little boy response," Maggie interjects. "I saw Jim go silent and into a moody state as soon as I said something about the trimming."

Jim continues by explaining that Maggie reacted by going into an opinionated mood and letting Jim have it. "There you go again. 'Oh poor me, the victim.' You sound just like your mother. Let me tell you, I'm not into pity and don't be so sensitive. The job has to be done, so it may as well be done right!"

They both knew they were on a track toward a destructive argument but neither could stop. "It was like we were possessed," Maggie added.

Ann, concerned, asks how they can avoid this.

Seeing Ann's concern, Maggie answers compassionately that it helps if they can catch themselves as soon as the mood hits. Then they can ask themselves what is going on before they pull the other partner in. They can also help each other. When Maggie saw Jim going into his moodiness, she admits that she could have softened a bit and become reassuring. When he muttered that nothing he did could satisfy her, Maggie could have said, 'That's not true, you do satisfy me and I love being with you working on projects together." Maggie observes that they were not talking about working together, anyway. What was coming up was much bigger than just trimming bushes and cleaning up.

Eager to own his part in the argument, Jim adds that he could have said that himself. He could have said to himself that he was going off the deep end and explained his struggle to Maggie instead of blaming her for his foul mood. He also recognizes that it is his responsibility to shift his own attitude and perspective.

People in the group are following the story intently. We begin by discussing how the situation could have gone the other way. Jim could have said something critical to Maggie about her approach to housekeeping, her appearance, her weight, or anything that could trigger a moody state in her.

Massimilla notes that being moody and opinionated and doing nothing about it can, over time, cause an irreversible split in a relationship. We also briefly mention that while both people can be either moody, opinionated, or both, it is beyond the scope of our seminar to go into more depth about this very complex dynamic. We announce that we will cover this ground in our next book, and in a more advanced seminar.

*Moody and Opinionated
Can Poison our Relationship*

Poisonous Cycles of Relating

I move on to describe how moody and opinionated are two states that can overcome us instantly if we are not careful. We need to know more about them if we want to stop them quickly and help each other. A moody state is marked by becoming withdrawn, passive, feeling deflated, afraid of conflict, being childish, over-sensitive, and resentful.

Massimilla continues by explaining that a moody state can quickly turn from just being grouchy to becoming very dark. If moody becomes dark, it can build resentment into passive aggressive behavior and eventually erupt in angry outbursts—from resentment to rage.

I use the example from the story to amplify the message. As Maggie and Jim discovered, these moods can sweep us away into an undertow before we know it. People generally feel sorry for themselves when they are caught in a moody state, but when pushed, small hurts become magnified and the person may become spiteful, petulant, and passive aggressive. For instance, if Jim had criticized Maggie for being too heavy, she could have gone into a moody state. When they sat down for dinner, if he continued to make negative comments about what and how much she was eating, she could have moved from hurt to anger, and then retaliated by criticizing him in a vicious manner.

Continuing to describe what happens when people are caught in an opinionated mood, I observe that they can become judgmental, critical, make general statements that do not fit the situation, and consider themselves the ultimate authority. In this condition we sound like a prosecutor, a commandant, a critical parent, or a snide, sarcastic know-it-all who tries to make our partner feel inferior, defeated, and guilty. If Jim considered himself well versed in physical fitness, we can easily imagine the superior tone he might use as he criticized Maggie's weight and eating habits.

Massimilla points out that we can also turn these states against ourselves. These unhealthy cycles usually start within our own mind and when we get too uncomfortable with this self-flagellation, we then blame our partner for our moodiness and dark feelings. For example, we can get caught in a mood of hopelessness or become the victim of our inner critic, which can also be very opinionated and relentlessly belittling of our efforts. If a partner is around and we are not careful, we will try to blame them for our mood instead of facing it as our own. If they are feeling vulnerable and defensive, a fight is imminent.

Tom remarks that he can identify with these moods, but wants to know what is behind them. Several others nod in agreement.

I reply that, strangely enough, the answer is usually simple. If the person in the moody state can understand and express what they are really feeling, a fight can be avoided. In most cases we are feeling hurt, angry, neglected, or bewildered, and are trying to deny it.

"You mean we're afraid of causing conflict or of being rejected?" Trish asks, and Tom interjects, "Or of appearing selfish or petty?"

I respond that the answer is yes to both questions. If Jim had been able to admit to himself that he was really disappointed about not playing golf and angry at having so many obligations, the outcome could have looked much different.

If we find ourselves spiraling into one of these moods, we can say to ourselves or write in our journals, "I am feeling or acting angry, hurt, sad. What I am really feeling is _____." We need to come up with the right words to fill in the blank, such as devalued, disrespected, unappreciated, taken for granted, not trusted, unloved, etc. I share an example that recently happened when Massimilla was late meeting me somewhere and had not phoned (as we have agreed to do if one of us is late). I slipped into a moody state very quickly. I needed to be able to say to her, "I'm angry." And, I needed for her to acknowledge my feelings of anger without being critical or defensive. She could have reacted and exploded, 'God, you are just like your father. You are always grumpy! Get a life!' If she had, instead of helping to create a respectful, loving place in which I could get in touch with what was really going on with me, it would have fueled my anger, and then look out! Bring out the gloves 'cause there's going to be a fight.

Instead, she said, "I am late and I can see that you are angry, and I can understand why." By saying this she did not put me down; she showed me that she understood. This made it possible for me to explain that I was angry because I felt like I had been treated disrespectfully. She helped me defuse my moody state so I then could hear her reasons or apology and we could go on to have a pleasant time. I need to emphasize that before we could move on, I had to recognize my true feeling and share them to avoid being trapped in the moody state. She had to be open to hearing my feelings of anger without taking them personally and retaliating. Both are hard to do but when we are honest and patient, we are giving a gift to our relationship.

Attention, patience, listening, and sharing ourselves helps diffuse difficult situation. We must be committed to keeping them in the context of love, respect, kindness, and trust. After all, we are relating to the person we love, and we need to always remember that.

I point out that Jim needed to share his feelings of disappointment thoughtfully, without blaming Maggie for them. Perhaps he could have said something along the lines of, "I really wanted to play golf today, but I know we need to get this done. Let's see if we can enjoy it instead of just making a job out of it."

Massimilla emphasizes that we need to try to change the mood we are in right now. But we can only change by first owning the mood as ours, expressing our feelings honestly, and then being willing to let go of our moodiness or opinionated-ness.

Tying into her thoughtful remarks, I add that if we are in an opinionated mood, something else is usually bothering us. If Jim had unreasonably criticized Maggie about her checkbook or charge accounts, she might ask him what is really bothering him. It could be that he is feeling overwhelmed by financial concerns, or feeling like he is facing them all alone.

Massimilla suggests, referring to our story again, that when Jim fell into his bad mood, Maggie could have headed off her opinionated reaction by saying instead, "It really makes me feel bad when I try to be helpful and you get upset." Massimilla insists that we have to look for ways not to be drawn into the other person's struggle in the first place, or how to head it off once it starts. This means we have to trust each other enough to share our feelings and talk about what's bothering us, even if we sound like we are complaining or being negative.

Defusing Strategies

1. Listen without judging, justifying, or criticizing.

2. Reflect back what the other person has expressed.

3. Do not take their criticism personally.

4. Quietly ask, "What is really going on between us here?"

Imaginary Relationships

Ann, busy taking notes, looks up and nods in agreement as Steve tells Maggie that she has given them a lot to think about.

Maggie thanks them and adds that there is more and she hopes it is not too overwhelming. The two states, moody and opinionated, can lead us into what their counselor calls "Imaginary Relationships," or relationships that are all in our head. "Suppose I want Jim to come to my book group with me one night," she continues. "He comes occasionally, like other spouses who aren't regular members. But on this night, I have to present and explain a controversial book. His presence would make me feel supported and more confident."

While Maggie is thinking about asking him to come, she says to herself, "I know Jim loves me and wants me to feel supported. I'm lucky to have such a good husband and I'm sure he will be glad to come." But then Maggie's thoughts spiral out of control. "What if he has other plans? He hasn't mentioned any. I know he will understand what I want. But sometimes he can be stubborn. In the past he has said, 'How many times have I told you I need my quiet time. I work all day and I've got to get myself back.' In fact there have been times he's refused to go to some important events. He's said, 'I've got a busy day tomorrow and I don't want to waste my time like this.'" Even when Maggie got upset, he still would not go with her.

But at the same time, Maggie thinks, "That's in the past. I like him for who he is. He could be more supportive, though. Other husbands are. Sometimes I feel being married to Jim is worse than being single. But this time I am really getting angry and by the time Jim gets home, I may be furious."

Maggie winces as she asks us if we get the picture. She starts thinking about asking Jim for support and instead of stopping there, she moves into an imaginary dialog that leaves her feeling angry and rejected. Jim has not even come home yet and she is possessed by her fears of not being loved and supported.

"It's like she has had a discussion with an imaginary me and never actually approached the real me," Jim reflects. "I do the same thing. I will want to do something, imagine she will criticize it, decide not to bring it up, and plummet into a bad mood as soon as I see her. Yet nothing real has transpired except the emergence of my old fears and insecurities."

Steve and Ann look at each other and burst into laughter as they realize how familiar this pattern is.

*Jim, smiling, too, adds that if they are going to respect and trust each other, they have to learn not to be **afraid** of dealing with the real person.*

After a short break Trish begins our discussion by saying that she thinks fear is an innate characteristic, particularly the fear of disapproval. "I've had it to some extent for as long as I can remember." Most heads around the room nod in agreement.

His arm around Cindy, Tom asserts that there is no doubt in his mind that he grew up learning to curb how he expressed himself because he was afraid of upsetting his parents.

"Or our teachers and other grown-ups," Cindy adds. She goes on to say that they were taught to make choices that got approval. This means they learned to be afraid to make choices that might provoke disapproval.

I note that Cindy is right. Our culture has taught us that relationships should be smooth and harmonious. Its ambience should be cheerful and positive. We have all bought into this model to some extent. So it is frightening to go against the norm because there are no guarantees we will not be banished by the tribe, or what we think is the tribe: our families, friends, and peer groups if we stir up trouble.

There is visible relief in the room.

I smile and continue, "Yet we know if we ignore problems in our relationship, they only get worse and our moods will overtake us. It almost seems like moody or opinionated is waiting in a closet ready to jump out and stir up trouble or provoke disapproval when we try to ignore things to keep the peace. I have found that if I am not careful, my resentment can come out as a hardball pitch instead of a gentle toss when I am trying to communicate."

"I think I know what you mean," Trish says. In her first marriage, she was aware something was wrong but kept trying to deny it. She was afraid of what it might mean. But she discovered the same way that Jim and Maggie did that being motivated by fear leads us to do the wrong things.

"The fear of intimacy, of being inadequate and criticized, led me into being seduced by paths that looked less threatening," Tom volunteers. Instead of facing his relationship, he began to believe making more money, buying a bigger house, or taking more vacations would make them happy.

Trish thought moving out of the city would do it.

Bob changed careers. "I sure wasn't thinking clearly. At the same time I began to expect more and more from sex. But I was more demanding and less willing to be romantic. Our bedroom became a battlefield." He was afraid of not being desirable, respected, valued, accepted, or appreciated.

Massimilla observes that most of us who have been through several relationships have visited that battlefield. Once we begin to think negatively about our relationship, it snowballs because fear erodes our ability to stay centered and to relate with love and respect.

"You're right," Leah responds. The more afraid she becomes the worse she acts. "I get clingy and manipulative. I know I'm driving Karen away, but I can't seem to stop."

Trish admits that she has two major fears: losing herself and not being loved. "I'm afraid I will give myself away or forget about my needs and values by trying too hard to make things work."

"I understand how being afraid of not being loved can cause you to want to avoid conflict and even give yourself away," Vanessa says. She wants to know what trying too hard to make things work means. Does it mean trying to have a relationship that meets your ideals instead of your needs?

Trish responds that meeting her ideals is not exactly the way she would put it. It is more like failing to meet the standards she got from somewhere years ago. Part of her longs to have an Ozzie and Harriet life even though she knows that was not real, even back in the fifties.

"I get scared when my relationship doesn't match the dreams I have nurtured," she continues. "It's painful to let the only images that seem inspiring and successful go, even though they are from the past and I know they are unrealistic. What else can I look to for hope?"

Massimilla explains that it is very difficult to let those images or those old dreams go when we have to replace them with new ideas. The story of Eros and Psyche gives us a new vision of the life of a relationship. So does seeing our relationships as a journey. We need these new visions and the tools we have been discussing to energize us and carry us forward into the future. They become our guideposts and our inspiration.

"I follow what you're saying," Michael says, "but the fear of rejection and of losing Vanessa are my biggest fears, not failing my ideals."

Karen responds, "Same here," and several people agree.

Michael says that he finds himself caught between thinking he can live happily by himself and feeling that if he commits fully to the relationship, Vanessa can hurt him in ways no one else can.

Wondering if she can let herself be fully open to intimacy is a question that continually haunts Karen. "I'm afraid it means being too vulnerable if Leah leaves or stops loving me."

Trish admits that she is afraid that she could end up with no one being there for her, no one loving her. That is how she ended up in her last relationship. "I had to begin to learn how to love myself. I still struggle with that but with Bob, I want to have a healthier, more fulfilling, relationship."

"That's great," Cory responds, amid a chorus of agreement.

Massimilla points out that we have just made the same important point we discussed earlier: facing our fears and bringing them out in the open changes them. I would bet many of us feel less threatened already. Plus, naming our fears and feeling less threatened makes it easier to pay attention to our partner, truly listen, be patient, and continue to share ourselves.

When we ask ourselves what we are afraid of and why, and then share this process with our partner or a close friend, it helps us learn more about ourselves. We can create enough distance from the issue to view it more objectively and to see options that we may miss if we are too close to the issue, or are trying to deny it. No matter what we are afraid of, ignoring issues in our relationship is the same as ignoring our partner. Our partner will sense this and begin to think he or she is not important to us.

Massimilla shares that our feelings inform us about what is happening in the relationship. If we never show our emotions, we will draw out our partner's anger and resentment because they will not have any way to gauge their importance to us. We need to share our genuine feelings in a related way in the context of intimate communication. If we do not, we are opening the door for moody and opinionated to walk in and take over.

Leah finds that having a little fear of losing her temper or of going too far helps keep her from saying hurtful things she cannot take back. "I want to be sure I keep respect and kindness primary in our relationship. Jim and Maggie knew that what they were doing was destructive but had gone so far they couldn't stop themselves."

"It seems like moody and opinionated are states we use to get revenge for hurt feelings, or for being ignored," Cory adds. "When either one of these catches me, I remember every way I've been hurt since the beginning of time."

Massimilla reminds us that if we deeply value our relationships, we have to seek to understand our fears and other feelings. Then we must commit ourselves to discuss them honestly.

I must admit that understanding myself is not always easy. "Sometimes I have to think about my moods and try to figure out the feelings behind them. Or write about them in my journal, or talk with Massimilla, a friend, or counselor when I am stuck."

Bob was so thoroughly trained to be sensitive to other people's opinions when he was growing up that he lost his ability to know what he is feeling. "It's been hard for me to figure out my feelings," Bob acknowledges. "But

Jim's and Maggie's point about being able to ask people to change is a good one. That gives me permission to accept what I feel and act on it."

Trish admits that if Bob were to sit down and respectfully but firmly tell her what he was angry or hurt about, she would feel a lot closer to him, and safer. "That doesn't mean I wouldn't initially be defensive or try to justify what I did. Or that I would like what he was saying, but I would feel like he cared a lot about our relationship."

Michael shares a situation that happened to them. A few days before, Vanessa and he were dressing to go to a party. He put on a new red shirt and a pair of blue pants. Vanessa came in and said, "You aren't going to wear that shirt are you?" Michael felt like a balloon that had been punctured. "I immediately lapsed into moodiness and didn't say a word. But I got her back during the party. I ignored her, drank too much, and flirted with other women."

Vanessa, looking upset, adds that they argued all the way home afterwards.

Barry asks if Michael wore the shirt anyway, and Michael admits that he did, and later felt stupid, like he had been defying his mother. "I know Vanessa is not my mother, but when I feel put down, it makes me feel rebellious."

Massimilla explains that moody and rebellious often go together. When we feel put down, we may also feel vulnerable and afraid of being dominated. If this reminds us of our childhood, we may respond to our partner as if they were a critical mother or father. There is not a very good future in that pattern. In a case like this it is helpful for Vanessa, or any of us, to listen until the fire dies down. Then we have changed the context of the situation and we can begin to gently toss the ball back and forth.

"For a long time Tom came home from work in a bad mood," Cindy observes. He was sarcastic and short tempered with her and with the children when they needed help with their college applications. Cindy felt like he was looking for a fight. "I tried to be patient until I couldn't stand it any more, and then I would explode. The fight was on."

Cindy tells us that this pattern was too hurtful to continue. So she decided to learn how to respond to him without taking his mood personally. She was committed to a new behavior but in the beginning, no matter what she tried, when she reached out she would get pulled into a fight anyway. Attempts to cheer him up did not work either; he remained distant and unresponsive, and Cindy felt rejected and afraid. It also made her wonder what it would be like when their children were no longer there as a buffer.

Tom responds that he felt overwhelmed, driven, and unappreciated at work and at home. Without knowing it, he felt like a victim and was seething with resentment and hostility.

"I was like a man possessed by an evil spirit, to use the words from our story," Tom continues. "I had no idea how upsetting this was to Cindy and the kids. They all felt insulted and neglected. "

Cindy says things took a big turn for the better last week after she sat down with Tom and said that they were going to try out the intimacy skills they had been learning. She told Tom how much she and the children loved him, yet he was hurting them more than she could stand. Cindy spoke so quietly and carefully to Tom that he could see how much pain she was in. He was deeply affected by her demeanor and really heard her. Instead of getting defensive, Tom knew Cindy was right. It was one of the worst moments in his life, and one of the best.

This was a moment that signaled real growth. Cindy reflects that it took a lot of courage for them to face this issue. Tom knew he had a lot of work in front of him, but he felt loved, not threatened. She had to figure out what mattered most and then be brave enough to speak honestly with Tom, not accusing or criticizing but simply telling him she had reached her limit and wanted them all to be treated better.

The room becomes quiet while we absorb this story.

Slowly, after we have had time to digest the power of what Tom and Cindy have shared, a slow smile spreads across Bob's face as he tells us that he lost the battle with Opinionated in his first marriage. He could tell immediately when his ex-wife got into one of those "I-know-how-everything-should-be-done" moods. "Her tone of voice would sound controlling and harsh. It didn't matter whether we were working on the budget or getting ready to go hiking. My response was to be very kind and sweet."

Grinning mischievously, Karen responds, "I'll bet that worked great."

"It never worked," Bob laments. "I felt taken advantage of." Beneath that kind façade, he became very resentful and began to make sarcastic remarks. Bob admits that he looked for things to criticize in a sneaky way, or excuses to ignore her and do what he wanted to without first discussing it with her. He has been working on ignoring that old voice inside him that tells him he has to be kind, no matter what. "Stopping that voice and being able to talk more honestly with Trish is vital to growing a healthy relationship. It is also the key to my self-respect."

Massimilla reflects that we make significant steps forward in our growth when we learn not to blame our partners when things go wrong. When we are able to back off and look at ourselves, we can see the part we are playing. Relationships can help us see the difference between the way we want to express ourselves and the way in which we actually are doing it.

I explain that I find it helpful to remember the kind of dance opinionated moods and moody states can get into with each other. Opinionated speaks with unquestionable authority and Moody resents authority. That is one reason we need to recognize them quickly, before we are dragged blindly into a conflict."

Leah laughs and reveals that when Karen gets into an opinionated mood, it is not hard to recognize. She is like a bulldozer, leveling everything in front of her. It is an aspect of Karen's amazing energy and appetite—until it is turned against Leah. When it happens, Leah finds it very hard to cope with. She says that she is like Bob; she tries to be patient and kind but she does not make a good martyr. She needs to feel like she is seen and respected.

Karen responds thoughtfully that she realizes Leah is right. "I am a go-getter and sometimes that aggressiveness can go the wrong way and be destructive. I can turn this mood against myself, too, and end up feeling awful." She thinks it would be a big help if both Leah and she could sit down with the one who is upset and quietly say, "Whoa, you're running all over me. What's going on?"

I agree and add that we often need some firm, but respectful, help to become aware of when these states start, and for ways to strengthen our ability to resist them. But when we try to help our partner, we must be clear about our purpose and remember what is most important. That will protect us from getting pulled into a clash of opinionated and moody states, or a battle of wills.

Bob thinks that we need to learn how to be firm and honest with ourselves, too. "I used to find myself in an imaginary relationship a lot. Driving home from work, I might want to go out to eat. Then I would imagine all the reasons Trish wouldn't want to go. Because I always had to be kind, I would acquiesce to her imagined objections and be in a moody state by the time I got home. By learning to be aware of this tendency, I can stop playing this imaginary game before I allow it to put me in a bad mood."

Michael notes that he has never thought about how his imaginary relationship affects his real relationship. This is an important insight. "Maybe I have imagined a bad marriage based on others I've seen. That doesn't give Vanessa and I a fair chance."

Final Wrap-up

Cory acknowledges that they both have found these discussions very helpful, but have noticed the group has not discussed other problems common to couples, such as sex, money, raising children, dealing with step-children, etc.

Because we are moving toward our final wrap-up as a group, I acknowledge that she is right and that it might be helpful to remember how Massimilla and I have structured the discussions. In the beginning, a relationship was defined as a journey. While we are on this journey we will have to face many challenges and difficulties. Without a doubt sex, money, children, and stepchildren often bring us face-to-face with huge challenges. We believe, however, that answers to problems in relationships lie more in the way we learn to deal with them than they do with the specific problem. We want to share some important tools of the craft, or the skills and resources, to deal with life's twists and turns in a way that helps us grow into a more loving life together.

Our know-how begins with learning the skills for intimate communication and how to apply them in an atmosphere of love, kindness, respect, and trust. Our confidence in this work expands as we learn how to understand and appreciate our differences. We become masters in this field when we learn how to avoid the pitfalls of fear, moody and opinionated states, and the danger of letting our relationships be imaginary rather than real.

Let us take sex for an example. Sex is not a one-time issue in our lives. Our sexuality changes during every phase of life, from puberty to mid-life, and beyond. Many outside events such as stress, job problems, business, illness, and other stressful situations affect it, too. We need to have the skills to deal with these challenges in whatever form they arise. We are traveling in new territory and when we, or our partner, get lost or encounter a stormy season, the skills we have learned in the craft of relationship will help us stay confident and hopeful by reminding us that we are only experiencing one phase of many in our journey.

Massimilla reminds us that the craft of relationship provides us with the structure and resources from which to nurture our love and respect for each other while we work through our problems. With this support we can discover outcomes that bring us closer to each other and that grows trust, respect, and appreciation.

The craft will carry us through most of the challenges we face. But if we get stuck we need to get help instead of hurting each other, as Jim and Maggie did. We must remember that love and growth are our most important values and should never be sacrificed to false pride and stubbornness.

Just as composers have to learn the scales and painters have to master paints and brushes, I emphasize that we all are in training. Mastering the craft of relationship prepares us for creating the kind of relationship that is ultimately very fulfilling, like a work of art, poetry, or music.

Trish is encouraged that following the guidelines of respect, kindness, and intimate communication is already drawing them closer together.

Even though they are new to this process and they make mistakes, Karen and Leah share that the skills have greatly helped them to renew their loving feelings towards each other.

The guidelines have given Barry reassurance that he no longer needs to walk fearfully around sensitive issues with Cory and the children; he can face their challenges with more confidence and honesty.

Michael wants to remember what Maggie said about the craft, that it is like learning to ride a bicycle. Once we have mastered it, we always will have a sense of security, confidence, and quiet joy. That is very encouraging to him.

Vanessa identifies with Ann's comment that she was discovering a new meaning for the word "commitment." Mastering the craft leads to trust. And trust commits our energy, minds, and hearts to creating a lasting relationship.

Massimilla and I always find the ending of our seminars moving. We have come to know these couples and it has been a rich experience. Several people exchange embraces. Many want to continue their discussions, and several hope they can share what they have learned with others, just as Maggie and Jim did.

We hope so, too, because we believe we are standing on the threshold of a new era in relationships. Having lived through several decades of statistics reminding us of how the old patterns are failing, we have witnessed the hurt and frustration of the ending to a painful cycle in history. And our new beginning is off to a strong start if we remember that the life of a relationship, like love, is a journey. Sustenance for this journey is found in respect and trust towards ourselves and towards the people we love. Intimate communication is the vehicle that can carry and sustain us. Appreciating our differences will bring a rich experience of the ways we add texture, meaning, and joy to each other's lives. Together our story grows into an ever-deepening awareness of love. Love as a journey promises us that we can grow together through our struggles and create the loving relationships we want, need, and desire. As in the story of Eros and Psyche, our challenges bravely confronted transform us and offer us both priceless gifts: who we become on the journey in our relationship, and a life worth being in together.

If love is the art, then relationship
is the craft of being in life together

Appendix A

Eros and Psyche[*]

Aphrodite, the goddess of love, was jealous and angry because a mortal princess named Psyche had become so famous for her beauty that mere mortals were beginning to say that she was even more lovely than Aphrodite herself.

Aphrodite sent her son Eros, the god of love, to shoot Psyche with one of his arrows, to make her fall in love with the most hideous monster he could find. But the girl's exquisite beauty so enchanted him that he could not bring himself to carry out his mother's command.

Meanwhile, the oracle of Apollo at Delphi had warned Psyche's father that she would never be the bride of an ordinary man, but rather would marry a being who flies through the night like a winged serpent, one whose power was so great that even Zeus, the king of the gods, could not withstand it. The king was told to take his daughter to the mountaintop and leave her there, and the wind would transport her to the abode of her husband.

The next morning, Psyche, her father and mother, and her two sisters made their way sadly to the top of the mountain. Tearfully they bade each other farewell, and then her family returned to the palace, leaving the frightened girl alone on the mountaintop.

As soon as she was quite alone, Psyche felt herself lifted by a gentle breeze, which carried her far away to a beautiful palace built of marble and richly decorated with gold, silver, and precious gems. When she went inside, she found that an elaborate wedding feast had been prepared, but she saw no guests. Invisible servants began to wait on her, and in soft voices they assured her that she was mistress of the palace, and that everything in it was hers.

That night her new husband came to her, but the palace was so completely dark that she could not see him. Still, he was kind and gentle, and his words were loving and sweet. She soon fell in love with him. He promised that he would give her anything she wanted, but warned her that she must never try to see his face. If ever she should look upon his face, they would have to part, and she would then live in loneliness and misery.

For many months Psyche was content to live with the husband she had come to love so dearly, but she never stopped missing her sisters. She began to plead with him to bring them to visit her. He warned her that they would cause trouble, but in the end he could not refuse his bride's request.

The next day, when Psyche's sisters went to the mountaintop, as they did every day, to weep over their lost sister, the wind lifted them and carried them to Psyche's new home. When they were set down before the gorgeous palace, the sisters felt amazed at such wealth. They were even more astonished when their lost sister ran out of the palace to greet them. She explained that the palace belonged to her new husband--and now, of course, to her as well.

Psyche's sisters could not help feeling jealous of Psyche's good fortune. They began to pry and probe, and to ask questions about her husband. Although she did not want to admit that she had never seen her husband's face, Psyche became confused and flustered under their relentless interrogation. In response to one question, she described him as having golden hair, as bright as the sun, but an hour later, she mentioned that his hair was as dark as night. These and other contradictory answers aroused her sisters' suspicion. They pounced on her errors, crying out, "Why, you have never even seen him, have you?"

When she finally admitted the truth, her sisters reminded her of Apollo's prophecy. It didn't take long for them to persuade the confused girl that her husband must be a terrible monster who would kill her as soon as he tired of her. They concocted a plan. Handing her an oil lamp and a dagger, they told her to wait until he was asleep, and then to light the lamp and steal a look at him. If he was, as they assumed, a terrible monster, then she would have to take the dagger and kill him.

That night, Psyche took the dagger from beneath her pillow and approached her sleeping husband. She lit the lamp and gazed for the first time on her husband's face, the face of the god of love! Instead of obeying his mother's command and making Psyche fall in love with a hideous monster, Eros had secretly taken her for his own bride. When she beheld the glory of Eros, Psyche was so startled that she allowed a drop of hot oil to land on his shoulder.

Awakened by the drop of oil on his shoulder, the god said sadly, "Where there is no trust there can be no love." Then he arose and left the palace.

Aphrodite soon learned that Eros had disobeyed her. She sought out his abandoned bride, determined to make her suffer. As soon as she found her, Aphrodite dumped a great pile of tiny seeds on the ground in front of the unhappy girl and ordered her to separate them--and to finish the job by sundown!

Looking at the enormous pile of seeds, Psyche knew that the task was impossible. It would take a hundred years to sort and separate so many seeds. But a large colony of ants, beguiled by the girl's beauty, decided to help her. Scurrying back and forth, they soon had the seeds sorted into separate piles. When Aphrodite returned and saw that the task had been completed, she became enraged and promised Psyche that her next task would be even harder.

She commanded Psyche to collect some wool from a herd of fierce man-eating sheep that lived in a thicket of thorn bushes near the river. Psyche knew it was certain death to approach the sheep, but as she drew near to the bushes where they lived, a voice told her to wait until evening, when the sheep would leave the thicket. Then she could collect the wool that had stuck to the thorns. Psyche did this, and once again Aphrodite was angry that Psyche had successfully completed a task that was meant to be impossible.

Aphrodite continued to set impossible tasks for Psyche, but somehow the girl kept managing to complete them. What neither Psyche nor Aphrodite realized was that Eros was still watching over Psyche, sending her help when she needed it.

Zeus was well aware of these events. Finally he decided that enough was enough. He decreed that Eros had proved his love for Psyche, and Psyche had proved her devotion, patience, and obedience. He said that since Eros had chosen as his bride a mortal, who could not reside with him on Mt. Olympus, there was only one course of action. Zeus would have to grant her immortality. Once Psyche had drunk the ambrosial nectar of the gods from the cup of immortality she ceased to be mortal. Aphrodite no longer felt jealous of her, for she had only resented the girl because she felt that mortals had no right to rival the gods. At last she bestowed her blessing on the union between her son and the beautiful princess who had become one of the immortals.

* This narration of the Greek myth of Eros and Psyche taken from:
  http://ny.essortment.com/erospsyche_rvde.htm

Also by Massimilla and Bud Harris

Like Gold Through Fire   ISBN 978-0-9810344-5-4

Also by Bud Harris

Resurrecting the Unicorn   ISBN 978-0-9810344-0-9

The Father Quest   ISBN 978-0-9810344-9-2

Sacred Selfishness   ISBN 978-1-9307225-1-4

The Fire and the Rose   ISBN 978-1-8886024-2-5

Read more about Bud and Massimilla, subscribe to Bud's newsletter and download a number of their lectures at:

www.budharris.com

Lightning Source UK Ltd.
Milton Keynes UK
UKOW050214020612

193806UK00001B/10/P